Copyright © 2023 by Aldous Leon

All rights reserved. No part of this book may be reproduced, stored in a retrieval system, or transmitted in any form or by any means, electronic, mechanical, photocopying, recording, or otherwise, without the express written permission of the author, except in the case of brief quotations embodied in critical articles and reviews.

This book is a work of non-fiction. The recipes, tips, and advice contained herein are based on the author's own experiences and knowledge. While every effort has been made to ensure the accuracy and completeness of the information contained in this book, the author and publisher make no warranties, either expressed or implied, regarding the contents.

Kindle and Paperback editions.

Cover photography and interior images are original and any unauthorized reproduction is strictly prohibited.

Published by Aldous Leon. Distributed by Amazon KDP.
Printed in the United States of America.

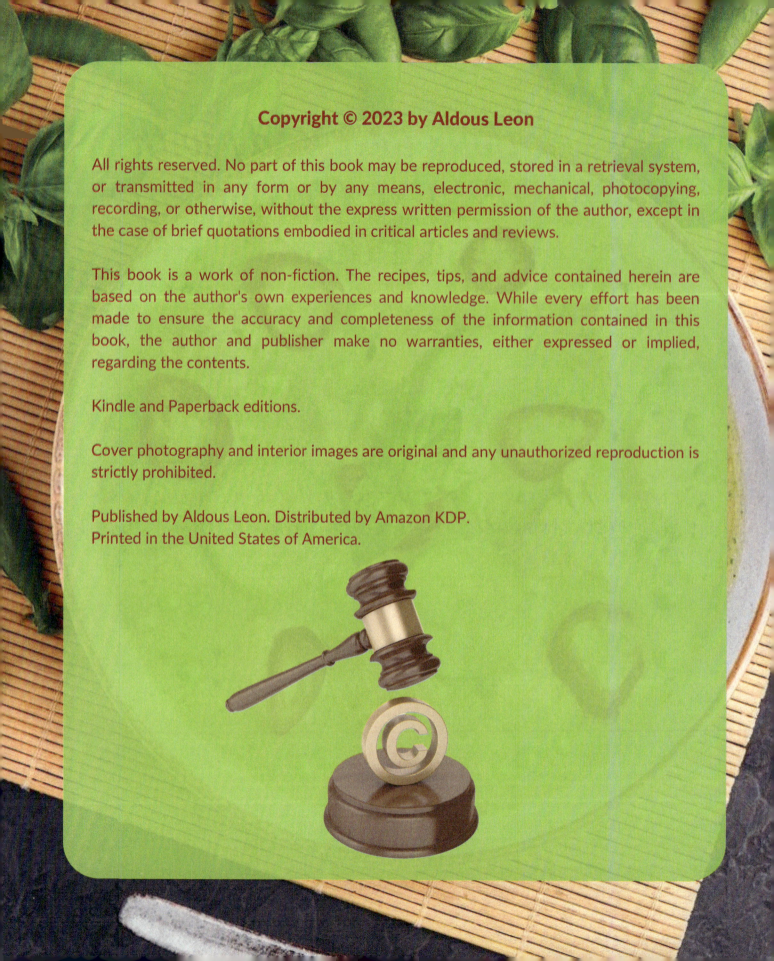

Contents

Introduction 04
- Importance of Protein for Muscle Gain
- How to Use This Cookbook
- Setting Yourself Up for Success
- Culinary Adventures Await

Chapter 1: The Basics of High Protein Diet 06
- Understanding Protein and its Role in Muscle Gain
- Benefits of a High Protein Diet
- Recommended Dietary Protein Intake
- Tips for Muscle Gain

Chapter 2: Getting Started 08
- Essential Kitchen Tools and Appliances
- Tips for Preparing High-Protein Meals
- Stocking Your Pantry with High Protein Ingredients

Chapter 3: Morning Muscle Fuel: High-Protein Breakfast Recipes 11

Chapter 4: Midday Muscle Meals: Lunch Recipes 37

Chapter 5: Evening Muscle Builders: High-Protein Dinner Recipes 63

Chapter 6: Protein-Infused Snacks & Sides: For Muscle Gain 89

Chapter 7: Muscle Building Indulgences: Desserts & Beverages 115

Chapter 8: Meal Plans and Fitness Tips 141
- Weekly Meal Plans
- Tips for Combining Exercise with a High-Protein Diet
- Tracking Your Progress
- Things to focus on for progress tracking

Conclusion 145

Introduction

Welcome to "Unlock Your Best Body with the High Protein Cookbook for Muscle Gain!" your one-stop resource for transforming your body and enhancing your muscle growth through nutritious and delicious high-protein recipes. Whether you are a fitness enthusiast aiming to push your limits or someone who is just starting out on a journey towards a healthier, stronger body, this book will guide you every step of the way. It's more than just a cookbook; it's a gateway to a new, healthier, and stronger you.

Importance of Protein for Muscle Gain

Before we dive into the delectable recipes that await you, it's essential to understand why protein plays a vital role in muscle gain. Protein, one of the three macronutrients, is the building block of muscles. It's composed of amino acids, which are essential in repairing muscle tissues that undergo wear and tear during workouts. Consuming an adequate amount of protein helps in fostering muscle growth, enhancing muscle recovery, and reducing muscle loss during weight loss.

Including a variety of protein sources in your diet not only aids in muscle development but also supports other crucial functions in the body, such as hormone regulation, immune response, and maintenance of healthy hair, skin, and nails. Embracing a high-protein diet means fueling your body with the right nutrients that foster muscle growth and overall well-being.

How to Use This Cookbook

Using this cookbook is as simple as it is enjoyable. We have structured it to serve both novices and seasoned cooks, providing a range of recipes that are both quick and easy to complex and indulgent. Each recipe comes with a comprehensive list of ingredients, step-by-step instructions, and original pictures to guide and inspire you.

To get the most out of this cookbook:

1. Start with the Basics: Begin with familiarizing yourself with the first two chapters, which lay the groundwork for understanding the high protein diet and preparing your kitchen.
2. Explore the Recipes: Navigate through the array of recipes we have provided for breakfast, lunch, dinner, and snacks. Experiment with different flavors and combinations to find what works best for you.
3. Plan Your Meals: Utilize the meal plans in Chapter 8 to plan your week ahead, ensuring you have a balanced intake of high-protein meals that cater to your muscle gain goals.
4. Document Your Journey: Make notes of your favorite recipes, track your progress, and don't hesitate to tweak recipes according to your preference.
5. Pair with Physical Activity: For optimal results, pair your high-protein diet with regular physical activity. Incorporate tips provided in the fitness section to complement your dietary efforts and accelerate your muscle gain.

Remember, the journey to unlocking your best body is a personal one, and this cookbook is designed to be your companion in achieving your goals. Let's embark on this journey of Culinary exploration and fitness transformation together!

Setting Yourself Up for Success

Before you jump into trying out the recipes, take some time to set yourself up for success.

1. **Understanding Your Nutritional Needs:** Consult with a healthcare provider or a nutritionist to understand your specific protein needs based on your body type, fitness level, and health goals.
2. **Incorporating Variety:** Ensure to incorporate a variety of protein sources, including lean meats, dairy, legumes, and nuts, to achieve a balanced and wholesome diet.
3. **Quality Matters:** Choose high-quality, fresh ingredients for your recipes. It not only enhances the flavor but also maximizes the nutritional benefits.
4. **Stay Hydrated:** Alongside maintaining a high-protein diet, remember to keep yourself well-hydrated. Water plays a crucial role in various bodily functions, including supporting metabolism and aiding in muscle recovery.
5. **Mindful Eating:** Adopt a mindful eating approach. Enjoy each meal without distractions, savoring the flavors and textures, which can enhance your dining experience and help in better digestion.

Culinary Adventures Await

Now that you are equipped with the knowledge and tips to navigate this cookbook, a culinary adventure of high-protein recipes awaits you. From the first rays of morning sunshine accompanied by nourishing breakfasts to fulfilling lunches and hearty dinners, this cookbook promises not only muscle gains but also a delightful gastronomic journey.

Through each chapter, you will discover recipes brimming with flavors and enriched with the goodness of protein. Each meal is a step towards building a stronger, healthier, and happier you. Embrace the journey with enthusiasm and joy. Remember, every great journey begins with the first step, and you are about to take a giant leap toward unlocking your best body.

So, roll up your sleeves, put on your chef's hat, and let's get cooking! Together, we will embark on a culinary journey that nourishes both the body and the soul, fostering a lifestyle that embodies health, vitality, and joy.

Here's to a stronger, healthier, happier you!

Welcome to "Unlock Your Best Body with the High Protein Cookbook for Muscle Gain!". Let the culinary adventure begin!

Chapter 1: The Basics of High Protein Diet

Understanding Protein and its Role in Muscle Gain

In the grand scheme of nutrition, proteins are often considered the building blocks of life. It's Composed of amino acids; proteins play a crucial role in almost all biological processes. For muscle gain, it is indispensable; it assists in repairing muscle tissue damaged during workouts, facilitating muscle growth, and increasing muscle mass.

Muscle growth occurs when the rate of muscle protein synthesis exceeds muscle protein breakdown. This is why adequate protein intake, combined with resistance training, can foster muscle growth. Understanding the role of protein in muscle gain is the cornerstone of effectively utilizing a high-protein diet to achieve your body's goals.

Benefits of a High Protein Diet and its Role in Muscle Gain

Embarking on a high-protein diet can offer a myriad of benefits, especially for individuals keen on muscle gain. Here are some potential benefits:

- Muscle preservation: A high intake of proteins can help in preserving lean muscle mass, especially when you are shedding weight.
- Appetite control: Proteins have a higher satiety value compared to carbs and fats, which can help in reducing overall calorie intake.
- Metabolic boost: A high-protein diet can potentially increase your metabolism, aiding in weight loss and improving body composition.
- Recovery: Proteins assist in faster recovery post-workout by aiding in the repair of muscle tissues.

Recommended Dietary Protein Intake

Determining the optimal amount of protein is crucial. While the recommended dietary allowance (RDA) for protein is 0.8 grams per kilogram of body weight for the general population, those looking to gain muscle mass should aim for a higher intake.

For muscle gain, a general guideline is to consume 1.6 to 2.2 grams of protein per kilogram of body weight. It is essential to note that individual needs can vary, and it is always recommended to consult with a healthcare provider or a certified nutritionist to personalize your dietary plans.

Tips for Muscle Gain

When it comes to muscle gain, merely increasing protein intake is not enough. Here are some tips to ensure that you are on the right track:

1. **Balanced diet:** Incorporate a balanced diet that includes a variety of nutrients, not just proteins.

2. **Consistent workout:** Adhere to a consistent workout routine that combines resistance and cardiovascular training.

3. **Hydration:** Stay hydrated to facilitate optimal metabolic reactions and muscle function.

4. **Quality sleep:** Ensure you get quality sleep, as it is during sleep that most muscle repair and growth occur.

5. **Stress management:** Manage stress levels, as high stress levels can potentially hinder muscle growth.

With the right knowledge and approach, a high-protein diet can be your ally in achieving significant muscle gain. Keep tuned to the subsequent chapters to discover delicious high-protein recipes that will aid you in your journey to muscle gain.

Chapter 2: Getting Started

Diving into a high-protein diet can be an exciting journey, but like any culinary adventure, having the right tools and ingredients will make the process smoother. This chapter explores the essential kitchen tools and appliances, tips for preparing high-protein meals, and stocking your pantry with the right ingredients.

Essential Kitchen Tools and Appliances

Blender: Ideal for protein smoothies and shakes, allowing you to combine protein powders, yogurts, fruits, and other ingredients seamlessly.

Food Processor: Useful for preparing homemade protein bars, nut butter, and specific high-protein snacks.

Quality Knives: A set of sharp knives will help cut meats and chop vegetables efficiently.

Measuring Cups and Spoons: Ensuring you're getting the right portion sizes is crucial, especially when tracking protein intake.

Non-stick Cookware: Helps in cooking without needing excessive oils or fats, preserving the protein content in foods.

Grill Pan or Barbecue Grill: Perfect for grilling high-protein foods like chicken, fish, and tofu.

Slow Cooker: These appliances can be a boon for preparing protein-rich stews, soups, and meats.

Instant Pot: These appliances can be a boon for preparing protein-rich stews, soups, and meats.

Silicone Kitchen Tongs: Durable, non-stick, and heat-resistant, these versatile utensils offer precise grip and control for effortless cooking and serving.

Oven mitts: It protects hands from burns by providing a heat-resistant barrier when handling hot cookware and bakeware.

Tips for Preparing High-Protein Meals

1. **Marinate in Advance:** Marinating meats can add flavor and tenderness, making them more enjoyable and easier to cook.
2. **Plan Ahead:** Batch cooking and meal planning can help ensure you always have high-protein options available.
3. **Incorporate Variety:** To avoid monotony, ensure that you're rotating between different protein sources, including poultry, meat, fish, legumes, and dairy.
4. **Use Spices:** Spices can enhance the taste of your dishes without adding unwanted calories.
5. **Opt for Whole Foods:** Whenever possible, prioritize whole foods over processed ones. For instance, full chicken breasts and over-processed chicken patties.

Stocking Your Pantry with High Protein Ingredients

A well-stocked pantry can be the key to whipping up high-protein meals on the go. Here are some staple ingredients to consider:

1. **Dry Goods:** Lentils, beans, quinoa, chickpeas, and whole grains are not only high in protein but also rich in fiber.

2. **Canned Goods:** Tuna, sardines, and salmon are excellent protein sources. Opt for those packed in water to keep calorie content in check.

3. **Protein Powders:** Whey, casein, pea, and soy protein powders can be versatile additions to smoothies, baked goods, or oatmeal.

4. **Seeds and Nuts:** Chia seeds, flaxseeds, almonds, and walnuts can be sprinkled onto various dishes for a protein boost.

 **5. Dairy and Alternatives:** Greek yogurt, cottage cheese, and milk (or fortified plant-based milk) can be high in protein.

 **6. Frozen Goods:** Stock up on frozen chicken breasts, fish filets, and even edamame for quick protein sources.

 **7. Eggs:** A versatile protein source, eggs can be incorporated into various dishes or eaten on their own

With these tips and essentials at hand, you're well on your way to mastering the high-protein culinary landscape. The next chapters will dive into specific recipes and meal ideas to keep your protein game solid and delicious.

Contents

Recipe 01: **Muscle Morning Protein Smoothie** 12

Recipe 02: **Power-Packed Spinach and Feta Omelette** 14

Recipe 03: **Morning Glory Protein Pancakes** 16

Recipe 04: **Chia Protein Overnight Oats** 18

Recipe 05: **High-Protein Blueberry Quinoa Muffins** 20

Recipe 06: **Scrambled eggs with herbs on wheat-rye crispy bread** .. 22

Recipe 07: **Chia Seed Protein Pudding with Fresh Berries** 24

Recipe 08: **Muscle Boosting Breakfast Burritos** 26

Recipe 09: **Lean Beef Breakfast Sausage Patties** 28

Recipe 10: **Vanilla Whey Protein Waffles** 30

Recipe 11: **Lean Muscle Avocado Toast with Turkey Bacon** 32

Recipe 12: **Chocolate Peanut Butter Protein Porridge** 34

Chapter 3: Morning Muscle Fuel: High-Protein Breakfast Recipes

1. Muscle Morning Protein Smoothie

Dive into your morning routine with this power-packed Muscle Morning Protein Smoothie, the ideal breakfast to fuel your day with a healthy dose of proteins. This nourishing drink will revitalize your body, priming your muscles for an active day.

- Serving 2
- Prepping Time 10 mins
- Cook Time 5 mins
- Difficulty Easy

Nutritional Facts (Per serving):

- Calories: 300
- Protein: 25g
- Fat: 8g
- Carbohydrates: 32g
- Fiber: 6g
- Sugar: 18g

Ingredients:

- 1 cup of Greek yogurt, unsweetened
- 1 banana, ripe
- 1/2 cup of mixed berries (strawberries, blueberries, and raspberries)
- 2 tablespoons of protein powder (vanilla or unflavored)
- 1 tablespoon of chia seeds
- 1 tablespoon of almond butter
- 1/2 cup of almond milk
- A pinch of cinnamon
- Ice cubes (as required)

Step-by-Step Preparation:

1. Place the Greek yogurt, banana, and mixed berries in the blender.
2. Add the mixture's protein powder, chia seeds, and almond butter.
3. Pour in the almond milk and blend until smooth and creamy.
4. Adjust the consistency with ice cubes if necessary and blend again.
5. Pour the smoothie into glasses and sprinkle a pinch of cinnamon on top for flavor.
6. Serve immediately and enjoy your nutrient-rich, muscle-fueling breakfast.

Storage Guidelines:

Store any leftover smoothie in an airtight container in the refrigerator for up to 24 hours. Since the smoothie contains fresh ingredients, it's best consumed immediately after preparation.

Reheating Guidelines:

Reheating is not advisable for this smoothie as it will degrade the flavor and nutritional value. If stored, stir or shake well before consumption. Adjust consistency with additional almond milk if necessary. Always check for freshness before drinking.

Recharge and refuel with the Muscle Morning Protein Smoothie, a perfect start to a day of physical activity and wellness. This well-balanced breakfast option promises a burst of delightful flavors and a generous supply of proteins to keep your muscles happy and healthy all morning.

2. Power-Packed Spinach and Feta Omelette

Jump-start your day with a Power-Packed Spinach and Feta Omelette designed to fuel your muscles for the day ahead. This hearty, high-protein breakfast, brimming with vitamins and minerals, will keep you full and energized, making your morning as productive as possible.

Serving: 2
Prepping Time: 10 mins
Cook Time: 10 mins
Difficulty: Easy

Nutritional Facts (Per serving):

- Calories: 280
- Protein: 20g
- Fat: 20g
- Carbohydrates: 6g
- Fiber: 2g
- Sugar: 3g

Ingredients:

- 4 large eggs
- 1 cup fresh spinach leaves, washed and chopped
- 1/2 cup feta cheese, crumbled
- 1/2 small red onion, finely chopped
- 1 tomato, diced
- 2 tablespoons olive oil
- 1 teaspoon garlic powder
- Salt and pepper to taste
- Fresh herbs (parsley or chives) for garnish, optional

Step-by-Step Preparation:

1. In a bowl, beat the eggs with salt, pepper, and garlic powder until well mixed.
2. Heat olive oil in a non-stick skillet over medium heat.
3. Add chopped onions and sauté until translucent, about 2-3 minutes.
4. Stir in the fresh spinach and cook until wilted, around 2 minutes.
5. Pour the egg mixture over the spinach and onions, spreading it evenly.
6. Sprinkle the diced tomatoes and crumbled feta cheese on top.
7. Cover the skillet and let it cook for 5-6 minutes until the eggs are set and slightly golden on the bottom.
8. Garnish with fresh herbs if desired, and serve hot.

Storage Guidelines:

Store any leftovers in an airtight container in the refrigerator for up to 1 day. Consuming the omelette as soon as possible is recommended for optimal taste and texture.

Reheating Guidelines:

Reheat the leftover omelette in a microwave-safe dish for 1 to 2 minutes on medium power or until heated. Alternatively, you can warm it in a skillet over medium heat, covering it to ensure even heating, for about 5 minutes. Always ensure it is heated thoroughly before consumption.

Embark on a day of muscle-building and energy-sustaining activities with the Power-Packed Spinach and Feta Omelette in your breakfast repertoire. This delightful dish not only meets your protein needs but also adds a vibrant burst of flavor and nutrition to your morning, ensuring a wholesome start to your day.

3. Morning Glory Protein Pancakes

Begin your morning with a boost of protein and delightful flavors with these natural ingredients: Protein Pancakes topped with berries and yogurt. This nourishing breakfast dish is not only an excellent source of energy but also a feast for your taste buds, setting a positive and vibrant tone for the day ahead.

Nutritional Facts (Per serving):
- Calories: 280
- Protein: 22g
- Fat: 5g
- Carbohydrates: 39g
- Fiber: 6g
- Sugar: 15g

Ingredients:
- 1 cup whole wheat flour
- 2 scoops protein powder (unflavored or vanilla)
- 2 ripe bananas, mashed
- 2 eggs
- 1 cup Greek yogurt (divided for batter and topping)
- 1 teaspoon baking powder
- 1/2 teaspoon ground cinnamon
- 1/4 teaspoon salt
- 1 cup mixed berries (strawberries, blueberries, and raspberries)
- 1 tablespoon honey or maple syrup (optional)
- Fresh mint leaves for garnish (optional)

Step-by-Step Preparation:

1. In a bowl, mix together the whole wheat flour, protein powder, baking powder, cinnamon, and salt.
2. In another bowl, whisk the eggs and combine with mashed bananas and half of the Greek yogurt.
3. Gradually incorporate the wet ingredients into the dry ingredients, forming a smooth batter.
4. Preheat a non-stick skillet over medium heat and lightly grease it.
5. Ladle portions of the batter onto the skillet to form pancakes, cooking for about 2-3 minutes on each side until golden.
6. Serve the pancakes warm, topped with the remaining Greek yogurt, mixed berries, and a drizzle of honey or maple syrup if desired.
7. Garnish with fresh mint leaves for a refreshing touch.

Storage Guidelines:

Place any leftover pancakes in an airtight container, separating them with parchment paper to prevent sticking. Store in the refrigerator for up to 2 days. You can freeze them for up to 2 weeks for more extended storage.

Reheating Guidelines:

- For best results, reheat the pancakes in a toaster or oven at 350°F (175°C) for 5-7 minutes or until warmed. If using a microwave, place the pancakes on a microwave-safe plate and heat on medium power for 1-2 minutes.
- If frozen, allow the pancakes to thaw in the refrigerator overnight before reheating.
- Top with Greek yogurt and berries after reheating for the freshest taste.

Welcome a day of energy and fulfillment with a plate of Protein Pancakes adorned with natural ingredients, berries, and yogurt. This breakfast dish not only promises a high-protein start but also brings a burst of natural sweetness and zest to your morning, paving the way for a vibrant and productive day ahead.

4. Chia Protein Overnight Oats

Embrace the morning sunshine with a bowl of Overnight Oats adorned with bananas and pecans sprinkled with chia seeds. This high-protein breakfast is not just a time-saver but also a powerhouse of nutrients, ensuring a fuelled and active start to your day, with every spoonful promising a burst of flavor and energy.

Serving: 2
Prepping Time: 10 mins (plus overnight soaking)
Cook Time: 0 mins
Difficulty: Easy

Nutritional Facts (Per serving):

- Calories: 320
- Protein: 10g
- Fat: 14g
- Carbohydrates: 42g
- Fiber: 8g
- Sugar: 15g

Ingredients:

- 1 cup old-fashioned oats
- 1.5 cups almond milk or any milk of choice
- 1 banana, sliced
- 1/4 cup pecans, chopped
- 2 tablespoons chia seeds
- 1 tablespoon honey or maple syrup
- 1/2 teaspoon cinnamon powder
- 1/4 teaspoon vanilla extract
- A pinch of salt

Step-by-Step Preparation:

1. In a bowl, combine the old-fashioned oats and almond milk, stirring well to mix.
2. Add in the cinnamon powder, vanilla extract, and a pinch of salt, blending well.
3. Stir in half of the sliced bananas and half of the chopped pecans.
4. Cover the bowl and refrigerate overnight to allow the flavors to meld and the oats to absorb the milk.
5. The next morning, give the oats a good stir and divide them into two serving bowls.
6. Top each bowl with the remaining banana slices, pecans, and a sprinkle of chia seeds.
7. Drizzle with honey or maple syrup for a touch of sweetness.
8. Serve cold and enjoy a nourishing breakfast.

Storage Guidelines:

You can store Overnight Oats in the refrigerator for up to 5 days. Ensure you cover the container tightly to retain freshness. Avoid adding banana slices and pecans if you plan to store them, as they may get soggy or lose their crunch over time. Instead, add these toppings fresh when you're ready to eat.

Reheating Guidelines:

Overnight Oats are best enjoyed cold and do not typically require reheating. However, if you prefer them to warm, transfer a serving to a microwave-safe bowl and heat for 1-2 minutes or until warmed to your liking. Add the banana slices, pecans, and additional toppings after reheating.

Greet the morning with the rejuvenating taste of Overnight Oats enhanced with banana and pecans, coupled with the crunch of chia seeds. This high-protein breakfast dish promises not only a hassle-free morning but also a nourishing start, equipping you with the right amount of energy and zest to tackle the day's adventures.

5. High-Protein Blueberry Quinoa Muffins

Begin your day with the delightful burst of blueberries paired with the goodness of quinoa in these High-Protein Blueberry Quinoa Muffins. Perfectly moist and packed with protein, these muffins are a brilliant way to fuel your muscles for a morning filled with energy and zest, combining health and taste in each bite.

- Serving 12
- Prepping Time 15 mins
- Cook Time 25 mins
- Difficulty Moderate

Nutritional Facts (Per serving):

- Calories: 165
- Protein: 6g
- Fat: 3g
- Carbohydrates: 30g
- Fiber: 3g
- Sugar: 13g

Ingredients:

- 1 cup cooked quinoa
- 1 cup whole wheat flour
- 1/2 cup Greek yogurt
- 1/2 cup honey or maple syrup
- 2 eggs
- 1 teaspoon vanilla extract
- 1/2 teaspoon baking soda
- 1/2 teaspoon baking powder
- 1/4 teaspoon salt
- 1 cup fresh blueberries
- Zest of 1 lemon
- 1 tablespoon chia seeds

Step-by-Step Preparation:

1. Preheat your oven to 350°F (175°C) and line a muffin tray with paper liners.
2. In a bowl, whisk together the Greek yogurt, honey, eggs, and vanilla extract until smooth.
3. In another bowl, combine the whole wheat flour, baking soda, baking powder, and salt.
4. Gradually mix the wet ingredients into the dry ingredients until just combined.
5. Fold in the cooked quinoa, lemon zest, and chia seeds.
6. Gently stir in the blueberries, making sure not to overmix to prevent the blueberries from bursting.
7. Divide the batter evenly among the prepared muffin cups.
8. Bake for 25 minutes or until a toothpick inserted into the center comes out clean.
9. Allow the muffins to cool in the tray for 5 minutes, then transfer to a wire rack to cool completely.

Storage Guidelines:

Store the cooled muffins in an airtight container at room temperature for up to 2 days. For more extended storage, refrigerate them for up to a week or freeze them for up to 3 months. If freezing, individually wrap each muffin in plastic wrap and store them in a large, airtight freezer bag to preserve freshness and prevent drying.

Reheating Guidelines:

For room-temperature or refrigerated muffins, you can reheat them in a microwave for 20-30 seconds until warm. If the muffins are frozen, allow them to thaw at room temperature or defrost them in the microwave before reheating. Alternatively, you can warm the muffins in a preheated oven at 350°F (175°C) for about 5-10 minutes.

Experience the joy of a nutritious and flavorful morning with these High-Protein Blueberry Quinoa Muffins. A fantastic choice for a wholesome breakfast, these muffins serve as the perfect fuel, injecting your morning with vitality and nourishment. Treat yourself to this delightful blend of sweet blueberries and hearty quinoa to start your day on the right note.

6. Scrambled Eggs With Herbs on Wheat-Rye Crispy Bread

Embrace the morning with the simple yet luxurious taste of Scrambled Eggs with Herbs, served on Wheat-Rye Crispy Bread. This high-protein breakfast is not just about filling your belly but filling your senses, blending classic flavors with a fresh herbaceous twist to give you a strong and flavorful start to the day.

Serving 4
Prepping Time 10 mins
Cook Time 5 mins
Difficulty Easy

Nutritional Facts (Per serving):
- Calories: 195
- Protein: 11g
- Fat: 9g
- Carbohydrates: 18g
- Fiber: 3g
- Sugar: 2g

Ingredients:
- 4 large eggs
- 4 slices of wheat-rye crispy bread
- 2 tablespoons milk or cream
- 1 tablespoon butter or olive oil
- 1/4 cup mixed fresh herbs (parsley, chives, dill), finely chopped
- Salt and freshly ground pepper to taste
- Freshly grated Parmesan or feta cheese (optional)

Step-by-Step Preparation:

1. In a bowl, whisk together the eggs, milk or cream, and a pinch of salt and pepper until well combined.
2. Heat butter or olive oil in a non-stick skillet over medium heat.
3. Pour the egg mixture into the skillet and let it sit undisturbed for a few moments until it starts to set around the edges.
4. Gently stir and scramble the eggs until they are mostly set but still slightly runny.
5. Stir in the finely chopped herbs and cook for another minute or until the eggs are fully set.
6. Divide the scrambled eggs among the wheat-rye crispy bread slices.
7. If desired, sprinkle with freshly grated Parmesan or crumbled feta cheese.
8. Serve immediately.

Storage Guidelines:

Scrambled eggs with herbs on crispy bread are best enjoyed fresh to maintain the texture and flavor of the dish. However, store the scrambled eggs and crispy bread separately if you have leftovers. Place the scrambled eggs in an airtight container and refrigerate for up to one day. Keep the crispy bread in a dry, cool place in a bread bin or another airtight container to prevent it from becoming stale.

Reheating Guidelines:

You can use a microwave or a stovetop to reheat the scrambled eggs. In a microwave, heat the eggs on medium power for 30 seconds to a minute, checking and stirring them every 30 seconds to prevent overcooking. On the stovetop, reheat the eggs over low heat in a non-stick skillet, stirring gently until warm. Be careful not to overheat, as eggs can become rubbery. Warm the crispy bread in an oven preheated to 350°F (175°C) for about 3-5 minutes or until it regains its crispness. Once both components are warmed, assemble the dish by placing the eggs on the bread and serving immediately.

Begin your day on a nourishing note with the Scrambled Eggs with Herbs on Wheat-Rye Crispy Bread. This high-protein breakfast champions the balance of rustic goodness and sophisticated flavors, making every bite a symphony of taste and nutrition. It's a classic reinvented, designed to fuel your muscles and delight your taste buds in equal measure.

7. Chia Seed Protein Pudding with Fresh Berries

Begin your day with the delightful Chia Seed Pudding adorned with a vibrant strawberry berry medley. This dish is a haven of nutrition and flavor, offering a great source of protein to fuel your morning activities. Experience the joy of a breakfast that is as pleasing to the palate as it is beneficial to your health.

Serving: 4
Prepping Time: 10 mins (plus overnight soaking)
Cook Time: 0 mins
Difficulty: Easy

Nutritional Facts (Per serving):
- Calories: 190
- Protein: 5g
- Fat: 8g
- Carbohydrates: 25g
- Fiber: 8g
- Sugar: 14g

Ingredients:

- 1/4 cup chia seeds
- 2 cups almond milk or coconut milk
- 1 teaspoon vanilla extract
- 2 tablespoons honey or maple syrup
- 1 cup fresh strawberries, sliced
- 1/2 cup mixed berries (blueberries, raspberries)
- Fresh mint leaves for garnish (optional)
- A pinch of salt

Step-by-Step Preparation:

1. In a bowl, whisk together the chia seeds and almond or coconut milk until well combined.
2. Stir in the vanilla extract, honey or maple syrup, and a pinch of salt.
3. Cover the bowl and refrigerate overnight to let the chia seeds absorb the liquid and swell, forming a pudding-like consistency.
4. The next morning, give the pudding a good stir to break up any clumps.
5. Divide the chia pudding into four serving bowls.
6. Top each serving with a generous helping of sliced strawberries and mixed berries.
7. Garnish with fresh mint leaves for a refreshing touch.
8. Serve cold and enjoy a vibrant and nutritious breakfast.

Storage Guidelines:

- Store any leftover chia seed pudding in an airtight container in the refrigerator for up to 5 days.
- Keep the fresh berry toppings separate from the pudding until ready to serve to prevent sogginess.

Reheating Guidelines:

This dish is best served cold and does not require reheating. Simply remove from the refrigerator, add your toppings, and enjoy! If the pudding thickens too much during storage, you can adjust the consistency by stirring in a bit more almond or coconut milk.

Embrace a morning filled with vitality as you savor the Chia Seed Pudding topped with a lively strawberry berry medley. This high-protein breakfast dish not only promises a delightful culinary experience but also ensures a healthy start to your day, bringing together nutrition and flavor in a refreshing morning treat that revitalizes your spirit for the day ahead.

8. Muscle Boosting Breakfast Burritos

Start your morning with a power-packed breakfast that satisfies your taste buds and fuels your muscles for the day ahead. These Muscle Boosting Breakfast Burritos are the perfect combination of protein, fiber, and essential nutrients to jumpstart your morning routine.

Serving: 4
Prepping Time: 15 mins
Cook Time: 20 mins
Difficulty: Easy

Nutritional Facts (Per serving):
- Calories: 520
- Protein: 28g
- Fat: 32g
- Carbohydrates: 34g
- Fiber: 8g
- Sodium: 680mg

Ingredients:

- 8 whole eggs, beaten
- 4 whole wheat tortillas
- 1 cup black beans, cooked
- 1 cup cheddar cheese, shredded
- 1 medium red bell pepper, diced
- 1 medium onion, diced
- 1 avocado, sliced
- 2 tablespoons olive oil
- Salt and pepper to taste
- A sprinkle of fresh cilantro (optional)

Step-by-Step Preparation:

1. In a non-stick skillet, heat olive oil over medium heat.
2. Add the diced onion and bell pepper, sautéing until translucent and soft.
3. In the same skillet, pour the beaten eggs and scramble until fully cooked.
4. Lay out the tortillas and evenly distribute the scrambled eggs among them.
5. Top the eggs with black beans, cheddar cheese, and a few slices of avocado.
6. Fold the tortillas into burritos, tucking in the sides as you roll.
7. Serve hot, garnished with a sprinkle of fresh cilantro if desired.

Storage Guidelines:
- Wrap leftover burritos individually in aluminum foil or plastic wrap and store them in the refrigerator for up to 2 days.
- For more extended storage, place the wrapped burritos in a resealable plastic bag and freeze them for up to a month.

Reheating Guidelines:
- For refrigerated burritos, reheat in a microwave for 1-2 minutes or a preheated oven at 350°F (175°C) for about 10-15 minutes.
- For frozen burritos, thaw overnight in the refrigerator before reheating or directly from frozen, increasing the reheating time as needed. Microwave on a microwave-safe plate covered with a damp paper towel or reheat in the oven until hot and thoroughly heated.

Indulge in the rich flavors and nourishing ingredients packed into these Muscle Boosting Breakfast Burritos, the ideal choice for anyone looking to add a wholesome touch to their muscle-building regimen. Whether you're heading to the gym or gearing up for a productive day, this breakfast will keep you energized and satisfied.

9. Lean Beef Breakfast Sausage Patties

Unearth the power of a protein-packed morning with these Lean Beef Breakfast Sausage Patties. Kickstart your day and fuel your muscles with a breakfast that is not only wholesome but delicious, too. Set a positive tone for the rest of the day with this hearty morning meal.

- Serving: 4
- Prepping Time: 15 mins
- Cook Time: 10 mins
- Difficulty: Easy

Nutritional Facts (Per serving):
- Calories: 210
- Protein: 26g
- Fat: 10g
- Carbohydrates: 2g
- Fiber: 0g
- Sugars: 0g

Ingredients:

- 500g lean ground beef
- 1 teaspoon sage, finely chopped
- 1 teaspoon thyme, finely chopped
- 1/2 teaspoon garlic powder
- 1/2 teaspoon onion powder
- 1/4 teaspoon nutmeg
- 1/4 teaspoon cayenne pepper (optional, for a spicy kick)
- Salt and pepper to taste
- 1 tablespoon olive oil

Step-by-Step Preparation:

1. In a large bowl, combine the ground beef, sage, thyme, garlic powder, onion powder, nutmeg, cayenne pepper (if using), salt, and pepper.
2. Mix the ingredients thoroughly until well combined.
3. Shape the mixture into 8 equal-sized patties.
4. Heat the olive oil in a large skillet over medium heat.
5. Place the patties in the skillet and cook for about 4-5 minutes on each side or until fully cooked and slightly crispy on the outside.
6. Remove the patties from the skillet and let them rest for a couple of minutes before serving.

Storage Guidelines:

- Allow the cooked patties to cool completely. Place them in a single layer on a tray or plate, ensuring they're not touching, and freeze for 1-2 hours.
- Once frozen, transfer the patties to a resealable plastic bag or an airtight container, separating layers with parchment paper to prevent sticking.
- Store in the refrigerator for up to 3 days or in the freezer for up to 2 months.

Reheating Guidelines:

- For refrigerated patties, reheat in a skillet over medium heat for 2-3 minutes on each side until heated.
- It's best to thaw frozen patties overnight in the refrigerator before reheating. If in a hurry, they can be reheated directly from frozen in a covered skillet over low-medium heat, turning occasionally, until thoroughly warmed. Alternatively, microwave them on a microwave-safe plate, covered with a damp paper towel, for 2-3 minutes or until hot, turning once halfway through.

Revolutionize your morning routine with these savory Lean Beef Breakfast Sausage Patties. Perfect for gaining that muscle mass, this high-protein morning fuel will leave you satiated and energized to tackle the day ahead. Make a batch during meal prep to have a quick, nutritious breakfast ready in no time!

10. Vanilla Whey Protein Waffles

Begin your day on a high note with these delightful Vanilla Whey Protein Waffles. These waffles are not just a treat for your taste buds but are also packed with protein, making them a fabulous choice for muscle gain. Elevate your breakfast game with this quick and nutritious recipe.

Nutritional Facts (Per serving):
- Calories: 250
- Protein: 20g
- Fat: 5g
- Carbohydrates: 28g
- Fiber: 4g
- Sugars: 5g

Ingredients:
- 1 cup whole wheat flour
- 2 scoops vanilla whey protein powder
- 1 tablespoon baking powder
- 1/2 teaspoon salt
- 2 large eggs
- 1 cup almond milk
- 1/4 cup unsweetened applesauce
- 1 teaspoon vanilla extract
- Cooking spray for greasing

Step-by-Step Preparation:

1. Preheat your waffle iron according to the manufacturer's instructions.
2. In a large bowl, whisk together the whole wheat flour, vanilla whey protein powder, baking powder, and salt.
3. In another bowl, beat the eggs and then stir in the almond milk, applesauce, and vanilla extract.
4. Gradually add the wet ingredients to the dry ingredients, stirring until just combined.
5. Lightly grease the waffle iron with cooking spray.
6. Pour the batter onto the preheated waffle iron, spreading it evenly.
7. Cook according to the waffle iron's instructions, usually for about 3-5 minutes, until golden and crisp.
8. Serve hot with your favorite toppings, such as fresh fruits, yogurt, or a drizzle of honey.

Storage Guidelines:

- Once the waffles have cooled completely, please place them in a single layer on a baking sheet to freeze. Freezing them first in a single layer prevents them from sticking together.
- After frozen, transfer the waffles into a zip-top freezer bag or an airtight container, placing sheets of parchment paper between each to prevent sticking.
- Properly stored, they will maintain the best quality for about 1 to 2 months but remain safe.

Reheating Guidelines:

- To reheat, you don't need to thaw the waffles. Pop them in a toaster or oven until they are heated through and crispy on the outside. It usually takes 2-3 minutes.
- Alternatively, you can reheat them in a conventional oven. Preheat the oven to 350°F (175°C), place the waffles in a single layer on a baking sheet, and heat for about 10 minutes or until warm and crispy.
- You can also use the microwave for a quick option, but this method won't retain the waffle's crispiness. Heat on high for approximately 1-2 minutes, checking every 30 seconds to ensure they don't overheat.

Indulge in a breakfast that is both delightful and nourishing with these Vanilla Whey Protein Waffles. With a high protein content, these waffles are your secret weapon to fuel muscle gain and sustain energy levels throughout the morning. Start your day with a smile and a hearty breakfast that doesn't compromise on flavor or nutrition!

11. Lean Muscle Avocado Toast with Turkey Bacon

Start your day right with this protein-packed avocado toast. Crunchy turkey bacon paired with creamy avocado and juicy tomato makes this a breakfast favorite that's not just delicious but also fuels your muscles for the day ahead.

Serving: 2
Prepping Time: 10 mins
Cook Time: 5 mins
Difficulty: Easy

Nutritional Facts (Per serving):

- Calories: 320
- Protein: 15g
- Carbohydrates: 30g
- Dietary Fiber: 8g
- Fat: 18g
- Sodium: 480mg

Ingredients:

- 4 slices of whole-grain bread
- 1 ripe avocado, pitted and mashed
- 4 slices of turkey bacon
- 1 medium-sized tomato, sliced
- Salt and pepper to taste
- Optional: chili flakes or fresh herbs for garnish

Step-by-Step Preparation:

1. Cook the turkey bacon in a non-stick skillet over medium heat until crispy, then set aside.
2. Toast the whole-grain bread slices.
3. Spread a generous amount of mashed avocado onto each toast slice.
4. Place a slice of turkey bacon on top of the avocado.
5. Add tomato slices, season with salt and pepper, and garnish if desired.

Storage Guidelines:

- Avocado toast with turkey bacon and tomato is best enjoyed fresh due to the avocado's tendency to brown and the toast's loss of crispness over time. However, if necessary, store each component separately in the refrigerator. Place the mashed avocado in an airtight container with plastic wrap directly on its surface to minimize browning. Store the cooked turkey bacon and tomato slices in separate airtight containers.

Reheating Guidelines:

- To reassemble, briefly reheat the turkey bacon in a skillet over medium heat or in a microwave until warm. Toast the bread slices if they have lost their crispness.
- Spread the avocado onto the toast, then add the warmed turkey bacon and tomato slices. Season with salt, pepper, and optional garnishes to taste.
- Note that reheating is not recommended for the avocado and tomato as it may alter their textures and flavors. These should be applied fresh to the warm toast and bacon for the best experience.
- For the best quality and food safety, remember to consume the stored components within 1 to 2 days.

Boost your morning routine with this high-protein breakfast that not only satisfies your taste buds but also contributes to lean muscle growth. With the perfect balance of macronutrients, this dish ensures you kick-start your day with the energy and nutrients your body craves.

12. Chocolate Peanut Butter Protein Porridge

Indulge in a breakfast that feels decadent but is packed with protein and nutrition. This Chocolate Peanut Butter Protein Porridge will make your mornings feel like a treat while ensuring your muscles get the fuel they need to power through the day.

Serving: 2
Prepping Time: 5 mins
Cook Time: 10 mins
Difficulty: Easy

Nutritional Facts (Per serving):
- Calories: 350
- Protein: 20g
- Carbohydrates: 45g
- Dietary Fiber: 7g
- Fat: 12g
- Sodium: 150mg

Ingredients:
- 1 cup rolled oats
- 2 cups almond milk (or any milk of choice)
- 2 tbsp cocoa powder
- 2 tbsp peanut butter
- 1 scoop of chocolate protein powder
- 1 tbsp honey or maple syrup (optional for sweetness)
- A pinch of salt
- Sliced bananas or berries for topping

Step-by-Step Preparation:

1. In a saucepan, bring almond milk to a low boil.
2. Add rolled oats and reduce heat to medium-low, stirring occasionally until the oats have softened.
3. Mix in cocoa powder, peanut butter, and protein powder until well combined.
4. Season with a pinch of salt and add honey or maple syrup if desired for added sweetness.
5. Serve in bowls, topped with sliced bananas or berries.

Storage Guidelines:

- Chocolate Peanut Butter Protein Porridge is best stored in the refrigerator if not consumed immediately. Place the cooled porridge in an airtight container to retain its moisture and prevent it from drying out. Add the toppings only when you're ready to consume to avoid sogginess.

Reheating Guidelines:

- Reheat the stored porridge in a saucepan over medium heat, adding a splash of milk to regain its creamy consistency if it has thickened while stored. You can also reheat it in the microwave in a microwave-safe container, stirring every 30 seconds until it reaches your preferred temperature.
- Once the porridge is warmed, add fresh toppings like sliced bananas or berries before serving.
- Ensure to consume the leftover porridge within 1-2 days for the best quality and taste.

Elevate your morning routine with a bowl of this creamy, chocolatey porridge. Not only does it offer a protein boost to kickstart muscle recovery and growth, but it also delivers an incredible taste that will make you eagerly anticipate breakfast time. Get the best of both worlds: flavor and fitness with every bite!

Note:

⭐⭐⭐⭐⭐ **Leave a Review** ⭐⭐⭐⭐⭐
As an independent author with a small marketing budget, reviews are my livelihood on this platform. If you enjoyed this book, I'd appreciate it if you could leave your honest feedback. I read EVERY single review because I love the feedback from MY readers!
If you do not know what to write, you can simply choose a star rating (one to five stars), which only takes a moment.

Thank you in advance for leaving a rating or review. We appreciate you!

1. **FIND** this book on Amazon
2. **SCROLL** down to the reviews
3. **SELECT**

Write a customer review

Chapter 4: Midday Muscle Meals: Lunch Recipes

Contents

Recipe 13: **Tuna and White Bean Protein Salad** 38

Recipe 14: **Grilled Chicken Caesar Salad Protein Bowl** 40

Recipe 15: **Green and Healthy Quinoa and Grain Bowls** 42

Recipe 16: **Muscle Building Beef and Broccoli Stir Fry** 44

Recipe 17: **Bulking Up Chickpea & Spinach Curry** 46

Recipe 18: **Protein-Packed Grilled Salmon Salad** 48

Recipe 19: **Lean Muscle Building Shrimp & Quinoa Bowl** 50

Recipe 20: **Chargrilled Chicken & Vegetable Skewers** 52

Recipe 21: **High-Protein Vegan Buddha Bowl** 54

Recipe 22: **Power-Packed Sweet Potato & Black Bean Salad** 56

Recipe 23: **Turkey and Quinoa Stuffed Peppers** 58

Recipe 24: **Zucchini Noodles with Shrimp Pesto** 60

13. Tuna and White Bean Protein Salad

Elevate your lunch game with this Tuna and White Bean Protein Salad. This dish combines protein-rich tuna and fiber-packed white beans, making it an ideal choice for those focused on muscle gain. Quick and easy to prepare, it's perfect for a wholesome midday meal.

Serving: 4
Prepping Time: 15 mins
Cook Time: 0 mins (no cooking required)
Difficulty: Easy

Nutritional Facts (Per serving):
- Calories: 280
- Protein: 25g
- Carbs: 20g
- Fat: 10g
- Fiber: 6g

Ingredients:
- 2 cans of tuna in water, drained
- 1 can of white beans, drained and rinsed
- 1 small red onion, finely chopped
- 1/2 cup cherry tomatoes, halved
- 1/4 cup olive oil
- Juice of 1 lemon
- Salt and pepper to taste
- Fresh parsley for garnish

Step-by-Step Preparation:

1. In a large bowl, combine the drained tuna and rinsed white beans.
2. Add the finely chopped red onion and halved cherry tomatoes to the bowl.
3. Whisk together the olive oil, lemon juice, salt, and pepper in a separate small bowl.
4. Pour the dressing over the tuna and bean mixture, mixing well to combine.
5. Garnish with fresh parsley before serving.

Storage Guidelines:

- Store the Tuna and White Bean Protein Salad in an airtight container in the refrigerator if not consumed immediately. This salad is best enjoyed cold and can be stored for up to 1-2 days. Avoid freezing the salad, as it can affect the texture of the ingredients.

Reheating Guidelines:

- This salad is designed to be eaten cold, so reheating is not recommended. If stored in the refrigerator, take it out and let it sit at room temperature for a few minutes if desired, then give it a good stir before serving. Add any additional fresh garnishes or seasonings to taste at this time.
- Enjoy this refreshing and nutritious salad as a quick and convenient lunch option that doesn't compromise on taste or nutritional value.

Wrap up your lunch hour on a high note with this nutritious Tuna and White Bean Protein Salad. Not only is it rich in protein and fiber, but it also offers a burst of flavors that will delight your palate. Perfect for meal prep, this dish is a powerhouse for muscle gain.

14. Grilled Chicken Caesar Salad Protein Bowl

Rev up your midday meal with this Grilled Chicken Caesar Salad with Cheese and Croutons. This classic dish gets a protein boost from tender grilled chicken, making it a go-to choice for those focused on muscle gain. Easy to prepare and satisfyingly crunchy, it's perfect for a nutritious lunch.

Serving: 4
Prepping Time: 20 mins
Cook Time: 15 mins
Difficulty: Easy

Nutritional Facts (Per serving):

- Calories: 420
- Protein: 35g
- Carbs: 22g
- Fat: 20g
- Fiber: 4g

Ingredients:

- 4 boneless, skinless chicken breasts
- 1 head of Romaine lettuce, chopped
- 1/2 cup Parmesan cheese, grated
- 1 cup croutons
- 1/2 cup Caesar dressing
- Salt and pepper to taste
- Olive oil for grilling

Step-by-Step Preparation:

1. Preheat the grill to medium-high heat and lightly oil the grates.
2. Season chicken breasts with salt and pepper.
3. Grill the chicken for 6-7 minutes per side or until fully cooked.
4. Slice the grilled chicken into strips.
5. Combine the chopped Romaine lettuce, chicken strips, croutons, and grated Parmesan cheese in a large bowl.
6. Drizzle Caesar dressing over the salad and toss well to combine.

Storage Guidelines:

- Store the Grilled Chicken Caesar Salad separately from the dressing to maintain the salad's freshness. Place the salad in an airtight container and store it in the refrigerator. The Caesar dressing should be stored in its own container, preferably airtight and refrigerated. When stored properly, the salad can last for 1-2 days in the refrigerator.

Reheating Guidelines:

- Ideally, the Grilled Chicken Caesar Salad is best enjoyed cold. However, if you prefer to reheat the chicken:
    1. Remove the chicken pieces from the salad.
    2. Heat them in a microwave for about 1-2 minutes or until warm.
    3. Return the warmed chicken to the salad or place atop freshly prepared lettuce.
    4. Add dressing and toss just before eating.
- For optimal taste, always add the dressing and toss the salad right before serving. This ensures that the croutons stay crunchy and the lettuce remains crisp. Enjoy your revitalizing lunch!

Wrap up your lunch hour with this protein-packed Grilled Chicken Caesar Salad with Cheese and Croutons. This dish offers both crunch and flavor, making it easy to stay on track with your muscle gain goals. Whether eating it fresh or prepping it for later, this salad delivers on taste and nutrition.

15. Green and Healthy Quinoa and Grain Bowls

Elevate your lunch routine with this Green and Healthy Grain Bowl featuring quinoa, butternut squash, kale, and roasted chickpeas. Packed with protein, fiber, and essential nutrients, this dish not only fuels muscle gain but also ensures you stay full and energized for the rest of the day.

- Serving: 4
- Prepping Time: 25 mins
- Cook Time: 30 mins
- Difficulty: Moderate

Nutritional Facts (Per serving):
- Calories: 410
- Protein: 15g
- Carbs: 58g
- Fat: 14g
- Fiber: 12g

Ingredients:

- 1 cup quinoa, rinsed and drained
- 2 cups butternut squash, cubed
- 1 can chickpeas, drained and rinsed
- 4 cups kale, washed and chopped
- 1/4 cup olive oil
- 1 tablespoon paprika
- Salt and pepper to taste
- 1 lemon for juice

Step-by-Step Preparation:

1. Preheat the oven to 400°F (200°C). Toss butternut squash and chickpeas in olive oil, paprika, salt, and pepper.
2. Spread the squash and chickpeas on a baking sheet and roast for 25-30 minutes, stirring halfway.
3. While the veggies are roasting, cook quinoa according to package instructions.
4. Sauté kale in a little olive oil until wilted.
5. Assemble the bowls: Layer quinoa at the bottom, then add the roasted butternut squash, chickpeas, and kale.
6. Drizzle with lemon juice and additional olive oil if desired.

Storage Guidelines:

- Once cooled, transfer the individual components (quinoa, roasted butternut squash, roasted chickpeas, and sautéed kale) to separate airtight containers. This step prevents the ingredients from becoming soggy and maintains their distinct flavors.
- Store in the refrigerator for up to 3 days for optimal freshness.
- Store lemon juice separately to add freshness when serving.

Reheating Guidelines:

- To reheat - it's best to warm the quinoa, butternut squash, and chickpeas together in a microwave-safe dish for 1-2 minutes or until heated through. You can also use a stovetop, placing them in a pan over medium heat, stirring occasionally.
- If you prefer, the sautéed kale can be warmed briefly in the microwave or given a quick re-sauté on the stove. However, many find it just as delicious cold or at room temperature.
- Once your ingredients are reheated, reassemble your bowl and finish by drizzling with fresh lemon juice and olive oil, if desired.
- Enjoy your revitalized Green and Healthy Grain Bowl, as tasty and nutritious as when first made!

Infuse your day with wholesome nutrition and culinary excitement with this Green and Healthy Grain Bowl. It's the perfect combination of taste, texture, and nutrients to help you power through your day while keeping your muscle-gain goals in check. Ideal for meal prep, this grain bowl is a versatile addition to your fitness-friendly menu.

16. Muscle Building Beef and Broccoli Stir Fry

Indulge in the classic comfort of Beef and Broccoli Stir Fry with Rice, amped up for muscle gain. This hearty dish features tender beef and nutritious broccoli, served over a bed of fluffy rice. Perfect for a filling and balanced lunch, this stir fry comes together quickly without skimping on flavor.

- Serving: 4
- Prepping Time: 15 mins
- Cook Time: 20 mins
- Difficulty: Easy

Nutritional Facts (Per serving):

- Calories: 460
- Protein: 32g
- Carbs: 42g
- Fat: 18g
- Fiber: 4g

Ingredients:

- 1 lb beef sirloin, thinly sliced
- 4 cups broccoli florets
- 2 cups cooked rice
- 1/4 cup soy sauce
- 2 tablespoons sesame oil
- 1 tablespoon cornstarch
- 1 teaspoon minced garlic
- 1 teaspoon minced ginger
- Salt and pepper to taste

Step-by-Step Preparation:

1. Heat sesame oil in a large skillet over medium-high heat.
2. Add minced garlic and ginger, sautéing until fragrant.
3. Add the sliced beef to the skillet, cooking until browned.
4. Mix soy sauce and cornstarch in a small bowl to create a sauce.
5. Add broccoli florets to the skillet, followed by the sauce.
6. Stir well to combine, cooking until broccoli is tender.
7. Serve hot over cooked rice.

Storage Guidelines:

- Allow the beef and broccoli stir fry to cool completely before storing.
- Place the stir fry in an airtight container and store it in the refrigerator. If you have cooked rice leftover, store it in a separate container to avoid it becoming soggy. The stir fry can be kept for up to 3 days in the refrigerator.
- For more extended storage, consider freezing the stir fry (without the rice) in a freezer-safe container for up to 2 months.

Reheating Guidelines:

- If reheating refrigerated stir fry, it can be warmed in the microwave for 2-3 minutes, stirring halfway through to ensure even heating. Alternatively, reheat it on the stove over medium heat until it is warmed, stirring occasionally.
- If reheating from frozen, allow the stir fry to thaw overnight in the refrigerator. Then, reheat using the microwave or stove method as described above.
- Reheat the rice separately, using a microwave or stove, adding a splash of water to prevent drying out.
- Combine the hot stir fry with the warm rice, and serve immediately.
- Ensure the dish is piping hot before consuming, and enjoy your tasty and nourishing Beef and Broccoli Stir Fry once again!

Turn your lunchtime into a savory escape with this Beef and Broccoli Stir Fry with Rice. A perfect mix of protein, fiber, and complex carbs, this dish supports your muscle-gain endeavors while tantalizing your taste buds. Easy to cook and even easier to enjoy, it's a wholesome choice for any fitness-focused individual.

17. Bulking Up Chickpea & Spinach Curry

Indulge in a plant-based powerhouse meal with this Bulking Up Chickpea & Spinach Curry. Rich in protein and fiber, this curry is a dream come true for those aiming to gain muscle. With a blend of aromatic spices and hearty ingredients, this dish promises both nutrition and flavor.

Serving: 4
Prepping Time: 20 mins
Cook Time: 25 mins
Difficulty: Easy

Nutritional Facts (Per serving):
- Calories: 380
- Protein: 15g
- Carbs: 40g
- Fat: 20g
- Fiber: 10g

Ingredients:

- 2 cans chickpeas, drained and rinsed
- 4 cups fresh spinach leaves
- 1 can of coconut milk
- 1 onion, chopped
- 2 cloves garlic, minced
- 1 tablespoon curry powder
- 1 teaspoon turmeric
- 1 teaspoon cumin
- Salt and pepper to taste
- 2 tablespoons olive oil

Step-by-Step Preparation:

1. Heat olive oil in a large skillet over medium heat.
2. Add chopped onion and minced garlic, sautéing until translucent.
3. Stir in curry powder, turmeric, and cumin.
4. Add drained chickpeas to the skillet, mixing well with the spices.
5. Pour in the coconut milk, bringing the mixture to a gentle simmer.
6. Add fresh spinach leaves, stirring until wilted.
7. Season with salt and pepper to taste.
8. Serve hot, optionally over rice or with naan bread.

Storage Guidelines:

- Once the chickpea and spinach curry have cooled to room temperature, transfer it to an airtight container.
- The curry can be stored in the refrigerator for up to 3-4 days.
- If you wish to keep it longer, it can be frozen in a freezer-safe container for up to 2 months.

Reheating Guidelines:

- For refrigerated curry: Transfer the desired portion to a microwave-safe dish and microwave for 2-3 minutes, stirring halfway to ensure even heating. Alternatively, you can reheat it in a saucepan on the stove over medium heat, stirring occasionally until hot.
- For frozen curry, It's best to thaw it in the refrigerator overnight. Once melted, follow the exact reheating instructions as above.
- If serving with rice or naan, make sure to heat those separately according to your preference.
- Always ensure the curry is hot throughout before consuming. Enjoy the aromatic and nutritious flavors of your Chickpea and spinach Curry once more!

Infuse your midday meal with the rich flavors and muscle-building nutrition of this Bulking Up Chickpea & Spinach Curry. Whether new to plant-based eating or a seasoned veteran, this dish is a convenient and delicious way to fuel your fitness goals. Perfect for meal prep or an immediate feast, it's versatile, hearty, and satisfying.

18. Protein-Packed Grilled Salmon Salad

Experience the perfect balance of lean protein and vibrant veggies with this Grilled Salmon Fish Fillet and Fresh Vegetable Salad. Ideal for those focused on muscle gain, this dish combines omega-3-rich salmon with a colorful assortment of vegetables. Quickly prepared and packed with nutrients, it's a fantastic choice for a midday meal.

Serving: 4
Prepping Time: 20 mins
Cook Time: 15 mins
Difficulty: Easy

Nutritional Facts (Per serving):
- Calories: 400
- Protein: 35g
- Carbs: 20g
- Fat: 20g
- Fiber: 4g

Ingredients:
- 4 salmon fillets
- 2 tablespoons olive oil
- Salt and pepper to taste
- 4 cups lettuce, washed and torn
- 2 large tomatoes, diced
- 1 red onion, thinly sliced
- 1 lemon, cut into wedges
- Dressing of choice

Step-by-Step Preparation:

1. Preheat the grill to medium-high heat.
2. Brush salmon fillets with olive oil, then season with salt and pepper.
3. Grill the salmon for 6-7 minutes per side or until cooked through.
4. Combine lettuce, diced tomatoes, and thinly sliced red onion in a large bowl.
5. Place the grilled salmon on top of the salad.
6. Drizzle with your choice of dressing and garnish with lemon wedges.

Storage Guidelines:

- Allow the grilled salmon and salad to cool to room temperature.
- Store the grilled salmon and salad separately in airtight containers for optimal freshness.
- The grilled salmon can be refrigerated for up to 2 days, while the salad (without dressing) should be consumed within 1-2 days for best quality.

Reheating Guidelines:

- To reheat the salmon, place it on a microwave-safe dish and microwave for 1-2 minutes, or until it reaches your desired temperature. Be cautious not to overheat as the salmon can become dry.
- Alternatively, you can reheat the salmon in a preheated oven at 350°F (175°C) for about 5-10 minutes.
- The salad should be served cold. Add the dressing to the salad just before serving to maintain the freshness and crunch of the vegetables.

Serving Suggestion:

- Arrange the cold salad on plates and place the reheated salmon fillets on top. Drizzle with dressing and serve with lemon wedges on the side.
- Always check the temperature of the salmon to ensure it's thoroughly heated before consuming. Enjoy your revitalized and delicious Grilled Salmon Salad!

Boost your midday muscle meals with this Grilled Salmon Fish Fillet and Fresh Vegetable Salad. Packed with protein and essential nutrients, this dish not only satisfies your taste buds but also supports your fitness journey. It's a wholesome and flavorful option that works equally well for immediate enjoyment or meal prep.

19. Lean Muscle Building Shrimp & Quinoa Bowl

Unleash the power of superfoods with this Lean Muscle Building Shrimp & Quinoa Bowl. Packed with protein from succulent shrimp and enriched with the goodness of quinoa, this dish is a complete meal in itself. It's quick to prepare, making it an excellent choice for a nutritious, muscle-building lunch.

Serving: 4
Prepping Time: 15 mins
Cook Time: 25 mins
Difficulty: Easy

Nutritional Facts (Per serving):
- Calories: 380
- Protein: 30g
- Carbs: 45g
- Fat: 10g
- Fiber: 5g

Ingredients:
- 1 cup quinoa, rinsed
- 2 cups water
- 1 lb shrimp, peeled and deveined
- 1 cup parsley, finely chopped
- 2 tablespoons olive oil
- 1 lemon, juiced
- Salt and pepper to taste

Step-by-Step Preparation:

1. Bring 2 cups of water to a boil in a medium pot, add the quinoa and simmer until cooked about 15 minutes.
2. Heat olive oil over medium-high heat in a separate pan and add shrimp.
3. Cook shrimp until pink, approximately 4-5 minutes, then remove from heat.
4. Combine cooked quinoa, shrimp, and finely chopped parsley in a large bowl.
5. Drizzle lemon juice over the mixture and season with salt and pepper.

Storage Guidelines:

- Allow the shrimp and quinoa bowl to cool to room temperature.
- Place the mixture in an airtight container and store it in the refrigerator.
- Consume the dish within 1-2 days for optimal freshness and quality.

Reheating Guidelines:

- To reheat the dish, transfer the desired portion to a microwave-safe container. Cover it lightly to retain moisture and microwave on medium power until the shrimp and quinoa are warmed through, usually around 2-3 minutes. Be careful not to overheat the shrimp, as they can become rubbery.
- Alternatively, you can reheat the dish in a covered skillet over medium heat on the stovetop. Add a small amount of water or broth to prevent drying out, and stir occasionally until the mixture is hot.

Serving Suggestion:

- Once reheated, give the dish a good stir. If needed, you can adjust the seasoning with additional salt, pepper, or lemon juice. Serve it warm and enjoy!
- Always ensure the dish reaches a safe internal temperature before consuming. Adjust the reheating time based on your appliance's power and the amount of food you're reheating.

Invigorate your lunchtime routine with this Lean Muscle Building Quinoa with Shrimp and Parsley Bowl. Not only is it rich in muscle-supporting protein, but it also boasts an array of essential nutrients. Whether you're dining in or packing it for later, this wholesome bowl promises to support your fitness goals deliciously.

20. Chargrilled Chicken & Vegetable Skewers

Savor the chargrilled goodness of these Chicken Skewers featuring a colorful mix of onion, tomatoes, champignon mushrooms, and arugula. This high-protein, low-carb dish is tailor-made for those pursuing muscle gain, offering a delicious way to meet your nutritional needs. It's a quick and satisfying option for a midday muscle meal.

Serving: 4
Prepping Time: 20 mins
Cook Time: 15 mins
Difficulty: Easy

Nutritional Facts (Per serving):
- Calories: 350
- Protein: 30g
- Carbs: 20g
- Fat: 16g
- Fiber: 4g

Ingredients:
- 1 lb chicken breast, cubed
- 1 large onion, cut into chunks
- 2 cups cherry tomatoes
- 1 cup champignon mushrooms
- 2 cups arugula leaves
- 2 tablespoons olive oil
- Salt and pepper to taste
- Wooden or metal skewers

Step-by-Step Preparation:
1. If using wooden skewers, soak them in water for at least 30 minutes.
2. Preheat the grill to medium-high heat.
3. Mix cubed chicken with olive oil, salt, and pepper in a bowl.
4. Assemble skewers by alternating chicken, onion, cherry tomatoes, and champignon mushrooms.

5. Place the assembled skewers on the grill.
6. Cook for 12-15 minutes, turning occasionally, until the chicken is cooked through.
7. Serve over a bed of arugula leaves.

Storage Guidelines:

- Once the skewers have cooled to room temperature, remove the chicken and vegetables from the skewers.
- Please place them in airtight containers and store them in the refrigerator.
- The skewers should be consumed within 1 to 2 days for the best quality and safety.

Reheating Guidelines:

- You can opt for the oven, stovetop, or microwave when ready to reheat.
- Preheat to 350°F (175°C) for the oven, place the chicken and vegetables in an oven-safe dish, and heat for about 10 to 15 minutes or until warmed through.
- On the stovetop, use a skillet over medium heat. Add a small amount of oil, then the chicken and vegetables, stirring occasionally until heated.
- If using a microwave, place the items in a microwave-safe container with a loose-fitting lid or cover with microwave-safe plastic wrap. Heat on medium power for 1 to 2 minutes, checking and stirring at 30-second intervals to ensure even heating.

Serving Suggestion:

- You may choose to re-skewer the items after reheating or serve them as is. Consider serving over fresh arugula or your salad greens of choice, with additional seasoning or dressing as desired.
- Always make sure the reheated food reaches a safe internal temperature before consuming. Adjust the reheating time based on your appliance's power and the amount of food you reheat.

Elevate your midday meal with these nutrient-packed Chargrilled Chicken Skewers. This dish strikes the perfect balance between protein and veggies, helping you meet your muscle gain goals. Whether you're enjoying this meal fresh off the grill or as part of your meal prep, its rich flavors and wholesome ingredients are sure to satisfy.

21. High-Protein Vegan Buddha Bowl

Nourish your body and fuel your muscles with this balanced Buddha Bowl, featuring a medley of brown rice, avocado, various vegetables, chickpeas, and walnuts. Packed with protein, fiber, and healthy fats, this dish serves as a one-bowl wonder for your midday muscle meal needs.

Serving: 4
Prepping Time: 30 mins
Cook Time: 20 mins
Difficulty: Easy

Nutritional Facts (Per serving):
- Calories: 420
- Protein: 15g
- Carbs: 60g
- Fat: 16g
- Fiber: 12g

Ingredients:
- 2 cups cooked brown rice
- 1 avocado, sliced
- 1 red pepper, sliced
- 1 large tomato, diced
- 1 cucumber, sliced
- 1 cup red cabbage, shredded
- 1 can chickpeas, drained and rinsed
- 4 cups fresh lettuce
- 1/2 cup walnuts, chopped
- Dressing of choice

Step-by-Step Preparation:
1. Cook the brown rice according to package instructions if not already prepared.
2. In large bowls, start by layering the cooked brown rice.
3. Arrange the sliced avocado, red pepper, diced tomato, and cucumber on top of the rice.
4. Add shredded red cabbage and rinsed chickpeas to the bowl.

5. Top with a bed of fresh lettuce and chopped walnuts.
6. Drizzle your choice of dressing over the ingredients.

Storage Guidelines:
- First, allow all components of the Buddha Bowl to cool to room temperature if they aren't already.
- It's advisable to store each ingredient separately to retain the freshness and texture of each component. Place them into individual airtight containers.
- Store the dressing separately to avoid the salad becoming soggy.
- The Buddha Bowl ingredients can be refrigerated for up to 3 to 4 days. However, consider consuming the avocado immediately for optimal freshness, as it may brown and lose texture over time.

Reheating Guidelines:
- The Buddha Bowl is typically enjoyed cold or at room temperature, so reheating is often optional.
- If you prefer the ingredients to be warm, consider lightly reheating the brown rice and chickpeas either in a microwave or on the stovetop. Be cautious not to overheat, as this may change the texture.
- Microwave: Place the rice and chickpeas in a microwave-safe container and heat for 1 to 2 minutes, stirring halfway to ensure even warming.
- Stovetop: Warm the rice and chickpeas in a skillet over medium heat for 2 to 3 minutes or until they reach your desired temperature.

Assembling and Serving:
- When ready to eat, reassemble the bowl by layering the rice first and then adding the other components as listed in the recipe.
- Drizzle the dressing on top just before serving to maintain the crispness and freshness of the vegetables.
- Always ensure your food is at the correct temperature before consuming. Adjust the reheating time as needed based on your appliance's specifications and the amount of food.

Elevate your midday meal game with this Buddha Bowl that's not only delectable but also perfectly aligned with your muscle-gain goals. It's a vibrant, nutritious, and satisfying option for lunch that covers all your nutritional bases, making it an excellent choice for health-conscious, busy individuals.

22. Power-Packed Sweet Potato & Black Bean Salad

Elevate your lunch experience with this Power-Packed Sweet Potato and Black Bean Salad. This dish combines the nutritional benefits of sweet potatoes, black beans, and pepitas to offer a protein-packed meal that aids muscle gain. Rich in flavors and textures, it's a vibrant choice for a wholesome midday meal.

Serving: 4
Prepping Time: 20 mins
Cook Time: 30 mins
Difficulty: Easy

Nutritional Facts (Per serving):
- Calories: 350
- Protein: 12g
- Carbs: 40g
- Fat: 18g
- Fiber: 10g

Ingredients:

- 2 large sweet potatoes, cubed
- 1 can black beans, drained and rinsed
- 1/2 cup pepitas (pumpkin seeds)
- 1 avocado, diced
- 4 cups mixed greens (spinach, arugula, etc.)
- 2 tablespoons olive oil
- Salt and pepper to taste
- Dressing of choice

Step-by-Step Preparation:

1. Preheat the oven to 400°F (200°C). Toss sweet potato cubes in olive oil, salt, and pepper.
2. Spread the sweet potatoes on a baking sheet and roast for 30 minutes or until tender.
3. Combine roasted sweet potatoes, black beans, and pepitas in a large bowl.
4. Add diced avocado and mixed greens to the bowl.

5. Drizzle your choice of dressing over the salad and toss to combine.

Storage Guidelines:
- Allow all cooked ingredients to cool completely to room temperature.
- For optimal freshness, store salad components separately in airtight containers. This step helps retain the texture and taste of each ingredient.
- Keep the dressing in a separate container to prevent the salad from becoming soggy.
- The salad components can be refrigerated for up to 3 to 4 days. Avocado might brown with time; consider adding it fresh when you're ready to eat the salad, if possible.

Reheating Guidelines:
- This salad is best enjoyed cold or at room temperature. Reheating is generally optional or recommended as it may compromise the freshness and texture of the ingredients.
- If you prefer warm sweet potatoes, you may reheat them in the microwave for 1-2 minutes or in an oven preheated to 350°F (175°C) until warmed through (approximately 10 minutes). Be sure to check and stir occasionally for even heating.

Assembling and Serving:
- When ready to serve, assemble the salad by combining the sweet potatoes, black beans, pepitas, avocado, and mixed greens in a large bowl.
- Drizzle with the dressing right before eating and toss gently to combine.
- Always check the temperature of the food before consumption, and adjust the reheating time as necessary depending on your appliance and the amount of food.

Indulge in a nutritionally balanced and flavor-rich experience with this Roasted Sweet Potato Black Bean Pepita Avocado Salad. The dish aligns perfectly with muscle-gain goals, offering a well-rounded blend of protein, healthy fats, and fiber. This salad adds a colorful, delicious twist to your fitness journey and is ideal for immediate enjoyment and meal prep.

23. Turkey and Quinoa Stuffed Peppers

Fuel your muscle-gain journey with these Turkey and Quinoa Stuffed Peppers. This high-protein dish combines lean turkey with nutrient-dense quinoa, offering a well-balanced meal in a colorful bell pepper package. Perfect for meal prep or an immediate lunch, it's a flavorful and fulfilling option.

Serving: 4
Prepping Time: 15 mins
Cook Time: 35 mins
Difficulty: Moderate

Nutritional Facts (Per serving):
- Calories: 350
- Protein: 28g
- Carbs: 30g
- Fat: 12g
- Fiber: 6g

Ingredients:
- 4 large bell peppers, halved and seeds removed
- 1 lb ground turkey
- 1 cup cooked quinoa
- 1 can diced tomatoes
- 1 onion, chopped
- 2 cloves garlic, minced
- 1 teaspoon paprika
- 1 teaspoon cumin
- Salt and pepper to taste
- 1 tablespoon olive oil

Step-by-Step Preparation:

1. Preheat the oven to 375°F (190°C).
2. In a skillet, heat olive oil and sauté onion and garlic until translucent.
3. Add ground turkey to the skillet and cook until browned.
4. Stir in cooked quinoa, diced tomatoes, paprika, cumin, salt, and pepper.
5. Fill each bell pepper half with the turkey-quinoa mixture.
6. Place the stuffed peppers in a baking dish and cover with foil.
7. Bake for 30-35 minutes or until the peppers are tender.

Storage Guidelines:

- Once the stuffed peppers have entirely cooled to room temperature, please place them in an airtight container.
- If storing multiple stuffed peppers, place a sheet of parchment paper between each layer to prevent them from sticking together.
- Store in the refrigerator for up to 3-4 days.

Reheating Guidelines:

- For reheating a single serving, you can use a microwave. Place the stuffed pepper on a microwave-safe dish, cover with a damp paper towel to keep the moisture in, and heat on medium power for 2-3 minutes or until the internal temperature reaches 165°F (74°C).
- For oven reheating, preheat the oven to 350°F (175°C). Place the stuffed peppers in an oven-safe dish covered with aluminum foil. Heat for approximately 15-20 minutes or until warmed through, reaching an internal temperature of 165°F (74°C).

Serving Suggestion:

- Serve the reheated stuffed peppers warm, possibly with a side salad or a dollop of sour cream or Greek yogurt on top for extra flavor.
- Always check the temperature of the food before consumption and adjust the reheating time as necessary, depending on your appliance and the amount of food being reheated.

Liven up your lunch menu with these nutrient-packed Turkey and Quinoa Stuffed Peppers. A perfect mix of protein, fiber, and vitamins, this dish is tailor-made for those seeking muscle gain. Whether you're enjoying it fresh from the oven or as a reheated meal-prep option, you're in for a satisfying, wholesome feast.

24. Zucchini Noodles with Shrimp Pesto

Dive into a delightful plate of zucchini noodles paired with juicy shrimp and a rich pesto sauce. This gluten-free alternative to traditional pasta packs a protein punch, making it a perfect muscle-building lunch option.

Nutritional Facts (Per serving):
- Calories: 305
- Carbohydrates: 10g
- Sugars: 6g
- Saturated Fat: 4g
- Sodium: 490 mg
- Protein: 22g
- Dietary Fiber: 3g
- Fat: 21g
- Cholesterol: 140 mg

Ingredients:

- 4 medium zucchinis, spiralized
- 20 large shrimp, peeled and deveined
- 1 cup basil pesto sauce
- 2 tbsp olive oil
- 2 cloves garlic, minced
- Salt and pepper, to taste
- 1/4 cup grated Parmesan cheese
- Lemon wedges for serving

Step-by-Step Preparation:

1. In a large skillet, heat olive oil over medium heat. Add garlic and sauté until fragrant.
2. Add the shrimp to the skillet and cook until pink on both sides.
3. Stir in the spiralized zucchini noodles and cook for 2-3 minutes until tender.
4. Lower the heat and stir in pesto sauce until everything is well-coated.
5. Season with salt and pepper, then serve topped with grated Parmesan and lemon wedges.

Storage Guidelines:

- Allow the dish to cool completely to room temperature.
- Place the cooled zucchini noodles and shrimp pesto in an airtight container.
- Store in the refrigerator for up to 1-2 days. Avoid keeping it longer, as zucchini noodles can release moisture and become soggy.

Reheating Guidelines:

- Reheating this dish on the stove is recommended for the best texture. Microwave reheating may cause the zucchini noodles to release more water and become overly soft.
- Heat a pan over medium heat and add the stored zucchini noodles and shrimp pesto.
- Stir gently and continuously until the dish is heated through. Be careful not to overcook as the shrimp can become rubbery and the noodles too soft.
- If the dish seems dry, consider adding a small amount of additional pesto or olive oil to refresh the flavors.

Serving Suggestion:

- Once reheated, consider adding a fresh squeeze of lemon, a sprinkle of Parmesan cheese, or some fresh basil on top for enhanced flavor.
- Remember always to check the temperature of the food, ensuring it has reached 165°F (74°C) before consumption. Adjust reheating time as needed depending on your specific appliance and the amount of food.

Let your taste buds revel in the harmonious blend of zesty pesto, tender shrimp, and fresh zucchini. It's a light yet fulfilling dish that supports your midday muscle gain goals without compromising on flavor.

Note:

⭐⭐⭐⭐⭐ **Leave a Review** ⭐⭐⭐⭐⭐

As an independent author with a small marketing budget, reviews are my livelihood on this platform. If you enjoyed this book, I'd appreciate it if you could leave your honest feedback. I read EVERY single review because I love the feedback from MY readers!

If you do not know what to write, you can simply choose a star rating (one to five stars), which only takes a moment.

Thank you in advance for leaving a rating or review. We appreciate you!

1. **FIND** this book on Amazon
2. **SCROLL** down to the reviews
3. **SELECT**

Write a customer review

Chapter 5: Evening Muscle Builders: High-Protein Dinner Recipes

Contents

Recipe 25: **Beef Steak with Chimichurri Sauce** 64

Recipe 26: **Traditional Spanish paella with seafood and chicken** .. 66

Recipe 27: **Garlic Butter Shrimp Pasta** 68

Recipe 28: **Lamb Chops with Rosemary and Garlic** 70

Recipe 29: **Miso Glazed Salmon with Bok Choy** 72

Recipe 30: **Lentil and Sausage Stew** 74

Recipe 31: **Spinach and Ricotta Stuffed Pasta Shells** 76

Recipe 32: **Moroccan Spiced Lamb Meatballs** 78

Recipe 33: **Grilled Tuna with Mango Salsa** 80

Recipe 34: **Stir-Fried Beef with Mushrooms and Bell Peppers** 82

Recipe 35: **Lemon Herb Grilled Tilapia** 84

Recipe 36: **Thai Green Curry with Chicken** 86

25. Beef Steak with Chimichurri Sauce

Savor the rich flavors of a juicy beef steak perfectly complemented by the zesty chimichurri sauce. This high-protein dinner dish not only satisfies the palate but also fuels muscle growth, making it a delightful choice for fitness enthusiasts.

Serving: 4
Prepping Time: 10 mins
Cook Time: 10-12 mins
Difficulty: Moderate

Nutritional Facts (Per serving):

- Calories: 520
- Carbohydrates: 2g
- Sugars: 0g
- Saturated Fat: 12g
- Sodium: 600mg
- Protein: 45g
- Dietary Fiber: 1g
- Fat: 36g
- Cholesterol: 120mg

Ingredients:

- 4 beef steaks (approx. 8 oz each)
- Salt and pepper, to taste
- 2 tbsp olive oil

For the chimichurri sauce:

- 1 cup fresh parsley, finely chopped
- 4 garlic cloves, minced
- 1/2 cup olive oil
- 2 tbsp red wine vinegar
- 1 tsp red pepper flakes
- Salt and pepper, to taste

Step-by-Step Preparation:

1. Season the steaks with salt and pepper on both sides.
2. In a skillet, heat olive oil over medium-high heat. Add the steaks and cook to your desired level of doneness.
3. For the chimichurri sauce, Combine all the sauce ingredients in a bowl and whisk until blended.
4. Serve the steaks hot, drizzled with chimichurri sauce.

Storage Guidelines:

- Allow the beef steak and chimichurri sauce to cool completely.
- It's recommended to store the chimichurri sauce separately from the steak to maintain the best texture and flavor of both components.
- Place the cooled steak in an airtight container and store it in the refrigerator for up to 3 days.
- Store the chimichurri sauce in a separate airtight container in the refrigerator. It can last up to a week.

Reheating Guidelines:

- For optimal flavor and texture, reheat the steak on the stove.
- Place the steak in a skillet over medium heat, warming it gently on both sides until it reaches your desired temperature. Avoid overcooking it during this process to maintain tenderness.
- The chimichurri sauce is best served cold or at room temperature. Simply remove it from the refrigerator and let it sit for a few minutes to take off the chill before serving.
- If you prefer your sauce warmer, you can lightly heat it in a saucepan over low heat until it's warm, stirring frequently.
- . Be cautious not to overheat it, as it may change the flavor and consistency of the sauce.

Serving Suggestion:

- Once both the steak and sauce are warmed, plate the steak and drizzle the chimichurri sauce over the top. Optionally, you can also serve the sauce on the side for dipping.
- For additional flavor and presentation, consider garnishing with fresh parsley or red pepper flakes.
- Before consumption, ensure the steak reaches an internal temperature of 165°F (74°C) for safe eating. Adjust the reheating time based on your appliance and the thickness of the steak.

End your day on a high note with this delectable beef steak infused with the vibrant flavors of chimichurri. It's a protein-packed dinner that ensures muscle repair and growth while offering a gourmet dining experience.

26. Traditional Spanish paella with seafood and chicken

Indulge in a delightful culinary journey with this traditional Spanish Paella, brimming with luscious seafood and succulent chicken. Each serving provides an ample protein boost, making this vibrant dish a winning choice for muscle building and a tantalizing dinner.

Serving: 6
Prepping Time: 20 mins
Cook Time: 45 mins
Difficulty: Intermediate

Nutritional Facts (Per serving):

- Calories: 520
- Carbohydrates: 52g
- Sugars: 4g
- Saturated Fat: 3.5g
- Sodium: 800mg
- Protein: 35g
- Dietary Fiber: 2g
- Fat: 16g
- Cholesterol: 140mg

Ingredients:

- 4 chicken thighs, bone-in
- 1 cup mixed seafood (shrimp, mussels, and calamari)
- 2 cups Arborio rice
- 4 cups chicken broth
- 1 cup white wine
- 1 onion, finely chopped
- 2 tomatoes, diced
- 1 red bell pepper, sliced
- 3 garlic cloves, minced
- 1 tsp smoked paprika
- 1/2 tsp saffron threads
- 3 tbsp olive oil
- Fresh parsley, chopped (for garnish)
- Lemon wedges (for serving)

Step-by-Step Preparation:
1. In a large paella pan or skillet, heat olive oil over medium heat. Add chicken thighs and cook until browned.
2. Add onion, garlic, bell pepper, and tomatoes to the pan. Cook until vegetables are softened.
3. Stir in Arborio rice, smoked paprika, and saffron.
4. Pour in chicken broth and white wine. Bring the mixture to a simmer.
5. Add mixed seafood to the pan. Cover and cook until the rice is tender and seafood is cooked through.
6. Garnish with fresh parsley and serve with lemon wedges.

Storage Guidelines:
- Allow the paella to cool to room temperature. Please do not leave it out for more than 2 hours to prevent the growth of harmful bacteria.
- Transfer the cooled paella to airtight containers, separating them into portion sizes if necessary.
- Store the paella in the refrigerator for up to 2 days. Due to the mixed seafood, keeping the dish for a more extended period is not advisable.

Reheating Guidelines:
- The best way to reheat paella is on the stove to retain the texture of the rice and prevent the seafood from becoming rubbery.
- Add a portion of the stored paella in a large skillet or the original paella pan.
- Warm over medium-low heat, stirring gently to heat the mixture evenly. You may add a splash of chicken broth or white wine to moisten the rice if it has dried out.
- Heat the paella until it reaches an internal temperature of at least 165°F (74°C) for safe consumption and the rice, chicken, and seafood are hot.

Serving Suggestion:
- Once reheated, remove the paella from the stove and let it sit for a minute or two.
- Before serving, garnish with additional fresh parsley and provide lemon wedges for squeezing over the top.
- Serve the paella warm, ensuring each plate receives a fair distribution of chicken, seafood, and rice.

Note:
- Reheating seafood can cause it to become overcooked and rubbery, so be careful not to overheat the dish. If you prefer, you can remove the seafood, reheat the rice and chicken, and then gently warm the seafood separately before combining them again to serve.
- Always check that reheated food is piping hot all the way through before serving.

Transport your taste buds to Spain with this hearty and flavorful paella, perfectly balancing seafood and chicken for a protein-rich feast. Ideal for those looking to build muscle, this paella promises a nutritious and satisfying dinner, bursting with traditional Spanish flavors.

27. Garlic Butter Shrimp Pasta

Savor the delightful combination of succulent shrimp and perfectly cooked pasta with this Garlic Butter Shrimp Pasta dish. This meal, rich in protein and bold flavors, serves as an ideal dinner for those seeking to build muscle while enjoying a gourmet dining experience.

- Serving: 4
- Prepping Time: 10 mins
- Cook Time: 20 mins
- Difficulty: Easy

Nutritional Facts (Per serving):

- Calories: 420
- Carbohydrates: 45g
- Sugars: 4g
- Saturated Fat: 7g
- Sodium: 350mg
- Protein: 30g
- Dietary Fiber: 3g
- Fat: 13g
- Cholesterol: 190mg

Ingredients:

- 8 oz fettuccine pasta
- 1 lb large shrimp, peeled and deveined
- 3 tbsp unsalted butter, divided
- 5 cloves garlic, minced
- 1 cup cherry tomatoes, halved
- 1/4 cup chicken broth
- 1 cup baby spinach
- Salt and pepper, to taste
- Grated Parmesan cheese for garnish
- Fresh parsley, chopped (for garnish)

Step-by-Step Preparation:
1. Cook the fettuccine according to package instructions, then drain and set aside.
2. In a large skillet over medium heat, melt 2 tablespoons of butter. Add shrimp and cook until pink.
3. Stir in garlic and cook for an additional 1-2 minutes.
4. Add tomatoes and chicken broth, bringing the mixture to a simmer.
5. Stir in spinach and cooked pasta, cooking until spinach is wilted.
6. Season with salt and pepper, then garnish with Parmesan and parsley before serving.

Storage Guidelines:
- Allow the pasta dish to cool to room temperature. Avoid leaving it out for more than 2 hours to prevent bacterial growth.
- Transfer the cooled pasta to an airtight container.
- Store in the refrigerator for up to 2-3 days.

Reheating Guidelines:
- The stovetop is recommended for reheating this dish to ensure even warming and to prevent the shrimp from becoming rubbery.
- Place the stored pasta in a skillet or pan.
- Warm over medium-low heat, stirring gently to heat the mixture evenly. If the pasta seems dry, add a chicken broth or water splash to regain moisture.
- Continue heating until the dish reaches an internal temperature of 165°F (74°C) and the shrimp and pasta are hot throughout.

Serving Suggestion:
- Once reheated, sprinkle with a bit more fresh parsley and grated Parmesan cheese for added flavor and presentation.
- Serve the pasta warm.

Note:
- Reheat only the portion you intend to consume to maintain the dish's quality. Repeated reheating can make the shrimp overcooked and rubbery.
- Always ensure the food is hot throughout before serving. Avoid overcooking the shrimp during the reheating process.

Delight in a meal that's as nutritious as it is flavorful with this Garlic Butter Shrimp Pasta. Its ample protein content supports muscle-building efforts, while the blend of shrimp, garlic, and butter creates a taste that's irresistible to the palate, making dinner both delightful and beneficial for your fitness journey.

28. Lamb Chops with Rosemary and Garlic

Relish the robust flavors of Lamb Chops with Rosemary and Garlic. This exquisite, protein-rich dish offers tender lamb chops seasoned with aromatic rosemary and garlic, making it a delightful, muscle-building dinner option.

Nutritional Facts (Per serving):
- Calories: 450
- Protein: 36g
- Carbohydrates: 2g
- Dietary Fiber: 1g
- Sugars: 0g
- Fat: 34g
- Saturated Fat: 13g
- Cholesterol: 110mg
- Sodium: 90mg

Ingredients:

- 8 lamb chops
- 4 cloves garlic, minced
- 2 tablespoons fresh rosemary leaves, chopped
- 2 tablespoons olive oil
- Salt and pepper, to taste
- Lemon wedges, for serving

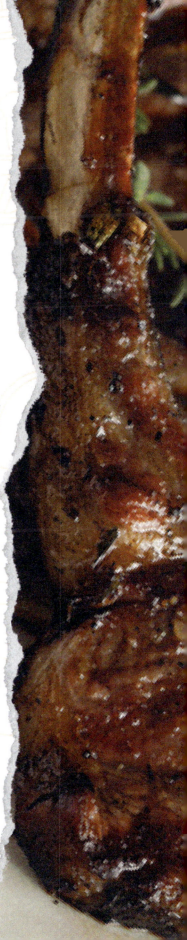

Step-by-Step Preparation:
1. Season lamb chops with salt, pepper, minced garlic, and rosemary.
2. Heat olive oil in a skillet over medium-high heat.
3. Place lamb chops in the skillet and cook for about 4-5 minutes on each side or until desired doneness.
4. Remove lamb chops from the skillet and let them rest for a few minutes before serving.
5. Serve warm with lemon wedges on the side.

Storage Guidelines:
- Allow the cooked lamb chops to cool to room temperature, but do not leave them out for more than 2 hours.
- Once cooled, place the lamb chops in an airtight container to prevent them from drying out.
- Store the container in the refrigerator for up to 3 days.

Reheating Guidelines:
- Reheating can be done either in the oven or on the stovetop, but the oven is recommended for an even heat distribution.
- If using an oven, preheat it to 375°F (190°C). Place the lamb chops on a baking tray and cover them with aluminum foil to retain moisture. Heat them about 10-15 minutes or until they reach an internal temperature of 165°F (74°C).
- Place the chops in a skillet with olive oil over medium heat for stovetop reheating. Warm them for about 2-3 minutes on each side, being careful not to overcook.

Serving Suggestion:
- After reheating, let the lamb chops rest for a few minutes before serving.
- Serve with fresh lemon wedges and additional rosemary sprigs for presentation and extra flavor if desired.

Note:
- It's essential not to overheat the lamb chops as they can become inflexible and lose their flavor.
- Always ensure the reheated meat reaches the safe internal temperature to consume.
- Consider reheating only the amount you plan to eat to avoid repeated heating and cooling cycles.

Experience the joy of a fine-dining meal right at home with these elegant and flavorful Lamb Chops with Rosemary and Garlic. Perfect for individuals on a muscle-gain diet, this dish promises a delightful burst of flavors while aiding your fitness goals.

29. Miso Glazed Salmon with Bok Choy

Experience a symphony of flavors with Miso Glazed Salmon with Bok Choy. A protein-packed dish, it promises succulence from the salmon, sweetness from the miso, and a delightful crunch from the bok choy, all perfectly complimenting your muscle-building dinner.

Serving: 4
Prepping Time: 20 mins
Cook Time: 25 mins
Difficulty: Moderate

Nutritional Facts (Per serving):

- Calories: 460
- Protein: 38g
- Carbohydrates: 40g
- Dietary Fiber: 3g
- Sugars: 4g
- Fat: 16g
- Saturated Fat: 3g
- Cholesterol: 70mg
- Sodium: 890mg

Ingredients:

- 4 salmon fillets
- 1/4 cup white miso paste
- 2 tablespoons soy sauce
- 1 tablespoon sesame oil
- 1 tablespoon mirin
- 2 cloves garlic, minced
- 4 baby bok choy, halved
- 2 cups cooked jasmine rice
- Sesame seeds and chopped scallions for garnish

Step-by-Step Preparation:

1. Preheat the oven to 400°F (200°C). In a bowl, combine miso, soy sauce, sesame oil, mirin, and garlic.
2. Place salmon and bok choy on a lined baking tray. Brush the salmon with the miso mixture.
3. Roast for 20-25 minutes until salmon is cooked and bok choy is tender.
4. Serve the miso-glazed salmon and bok choy over cooked jasmine rice and garnish with sesame seeds and scallions.

Storage Guidelines:
- After the dish has cooled to room temperature, transfer the salmon and bok choy to an airtight container, ensuring they are not overcrowded to maintain their texture.
- Store the cooked jasmine rice in a separate airtight container to prevent it from becoming soggy.
- Refrigerate both containers promptly. They will remain fresh for up to 2 days.

Reheating Guidelines:
- **Oven Method (Preferred for Salmon):**
1. Preheat the oven to 325°F (165°C).
2. Place the salmon and bok choy on a baking tray, ensuring they're spread out evenly.
3. Reheat for 10-12 minutes or until the salmon is warmed. Avoid overcooking, as this can dry out the salmon.
- **Microwave Method (Preferred for Rice):**
1. Place the rice in a microwave-safe dish and sprinkle a few drops of water to prevent drying out.
2. Cover the dish loosely with a microwave-safe lid or plastic wrap.
3. Microwave the rice on medium power for 1-2 minutes or until it's heated through, stirring halfway for even warmth.

Serving Suggestion:
- Once reheated, plate the salmon and bok choy over the jasmine rice.
- Garnish with a sprinkle of sesame seeds and freshly chopped scallions for added flavor and a fresh look.

Note:
- It's best to reheat only the portion you're going to consume to maintain the dish's flavor and texture.
- Always ensure that reheated food reaches a safe internal temperature before consuming.
- Try to consume the dish within the storage guidelines provided for optimum taste.

Dive into a well-balanced, flavorful meal that supports your muscle gain endeavor with a significant dose of protein. The harmonious blend of miso-glazed salmon, crispy bok choy, and fragrant jasmine rice makes each bite a delightful experience, offering not just taste but also nutritional richness.

30. Lentil and Sausage Stew

Dive into the hearty and savory world of Lentil and Sausage Stew. This protein-dense dish not only provides the warmth of a home-cooked meal but is also a powerhouse of nutrients essential for building muscles, making it an ideal dinner choice.

Serving: 6
Prepping Time: 15 mins
Cook Time: 45 mins
Difficulty: Easy

Nutritional Facts (Per serving):
- Calories: 540
- Carbohydrates: 56g
- Sugars: 6g
- Saturated Fat: 7g
- Sodium: 1230mg
- Protein: 32g
- Dietary Fiber: 24g
- Fat: 22g
- Cholesterol: 50mg

Ingredients:

- 1 lb smoked sausage, sliced
- 2 cups dry lentils, rinsed and drained
- 1 large onion, chopped
- 3 carrots, peeled and sliced
- 3 cloves garlic, minced
- 1 can (14.5 oz) diced tomatoes
- 8 cups chicken broth
- 1 teaspoon dried thyme
- 1 bay leaf
- Salt and pepper, to taste
- Chopped fresh parsley for garnish

Step-by-Step Preparation:

1. In a large pot, sauté sausage slices until browned. Remove and set aside.
2. In the same pot, add onions, carrots, and garlic, sautéing until softened.
3. Add lentils, diced tomatoes, chicken broth, thyme, and bay leaf to the pot.
4. Return the sausage to the pot and bring the mixture to a boil.
5. Reduce heat and simmer for 35-40 minutes until lentils are tender.
6. Season with salt and pepper, then garnish with fresh parsley before serving.

Storage Guidelines:
- Allow the stew to cool to room temperature before transferring it to storage.
- Pour the stew into an airtight container or multiple smaller containers if you prefer portioned meals.
- The stew can be refrigerated for up to 4 days.

Reheating Guidelines:
- **Stovetop Method (Preferred):**
  1. Transfer the desired amount of stew into a pot.
  2. Reheat over medium heat, stirring occasionally, until the stew is heated through. This step usually takes about 5-7 minutes.
- **Microwave Method:**
  1. Place a portion of the stew in a microwave-safe dish.
  2. Cover the dish loosely with a microwave-safe lid or plastic wrap.
  3. Heat on medium power for 2-3 minutes, stirring halfway to ensure even reheating. If necessary, continue to heat in 1-minute intervals until the stew is hot.

Serving Suggestion:
- Give the stew a good stir before serving to combine all the flavors.
- Garnish with some freshly chopped parsley for added freshness and a pop of color.

Note:
- Always make sure the reheated stew reaches a safe internal temperature before consuming.
- It's recommended to reheat only the portion of the stew you plan to eat to maintain its flavor and texture.

With each spoonful of Lentil and Sausage Stew, enjoy a burst of flavors and proteins that not only delight the palate but also contribute significantly to muscle building. It's the comfort of a homely, hearty stew coupled with the benefits of a high-protein dinner.

31. Spinach and Ricotta Stuffed Pasta Shells

Delight in the creamy and savory Spinach and Ricotta Stuffed Pasta Shells, a dish where each bite offers a burst of flavor and a dose of protein. This enticing dinner option is not only pleasing to the palate but also supports muscle-building efforts with its high protein content.

Serving: 6
Prepping Time: 20 mins
Cook Time: 30 mins
Difficulty: Moderate

Nutritional Facts (Per serving):
- Calories: 330
- Carbohydrates: 35g
- Sugars: 6g
- Saturated Fat: 7g
- Sodium: 650mg
- Protein: 18g
- Dietary Fiber: 3g
- Fat: 14g
- Cholesterol: 65mg

Ingredients:
- 24 jumbo pasta shells
- 1 tablespoon olive oil
- 2 cups ricotta cheese
- 1 cup fresh spinach, chopped
- 1/2 cup grated Parmesan cheese
- 1 egg
- 2 cloves garlic, minced
- 2 cups marinara sauce
- Salt and pepper, to taste
- Fresh basil for garnish

Step-by-Step Preparation:
1. Cook pasta shells according to package instructions, drain, and set aside.
2. Preheat oven to 375°F (190°C). In a bowl, combine ricotta, spinach, Parmesan, egg, garlic, salt, and pepper.
3. Spread marinara sauce in the bottom of a baking dish.
4. Stuff each pasta shell with the ricotta mixture and place in the baking dish.
5. Bake for 30 minutes or until heated through. Garnish with fresh basil before serv

Storage Guidelines:
- Allow the stuffed pasta shells to cool to room temperature after baking.
- Transfer any leftover shells and sauce to an airtight container or a baking dish with an airtight lid.
- Store the container in the refrigerator.
- The stuffed pasta shells can be refrigerated for up to 3-4 days.

Reheating Guidelines:
- **Oven Method (Preferred):**
1. Preheat your oven to 350°F (175°C).
2. Transfer the desired number of stuffed pasta shells to an oven-safe dish.
3. Cover the dish with aluminum foil to prevent drying.
4. Bake for approximately 15-20 minutes or until the shells are heated through.

- **Microwave Method (Quicker, but may result in softer pasta):**
1. Place a portion of the stuffed pasta shells on a microwave-safe plate.
2. Cover the plate with a microwave-safe lid or plastic wrap, leaving a small vent to allow steam to escape.
3. Microwave on medium power for 1-2 minutes, checking to see if they are heated through. You may need to microwave in additional 30-second intervals as needed.

Serving Suggestion:
- If desired, you can serve the reheated stuffed pasta shells with a drizzle of additional marinara sauce.
- Garnish with fresh basil or grated Parmesan cheese to add extra flavor and freshness.

Relish the rich, comforting flavors of Spinach and Ricotta Stuffed Pasta Shells that promise not only a delightful dining experience but also a high-protein meal beneficial for those looking to gain muscle. Every bite is a perfect blend of creamy, cheesy goodness and the wholesome goodness of spinach.

Enjoy your creamy and savory Spinach and Ricotta Stuffed Pasta Shells!

32. Moroccan Spiced Lamb Meatballs

Indulge in the exotic flavors of Moroccan Spiced Lamb Meatballs, a dish that blends rich spices with tender lamb for a high-protein, mouth-watering meal. Perfect for muscle building, these meatballs offer a delicious way to meet your protein needs while tantalizing your taste buds.

Serving 4
Prepping Time 15 mins
Cook Time 20 mins
Difficulty Moderate

Nutritional Facts (Per serving):

- Calories: 420
- Carbohydrates: 15g
- Sugars: 2g
- Saturated Fat: 12g
- Sodium: 330mg
- Protein: 22g
- Dietary Fiber: 1g
- Fat: 30g
- Cholesterol: 110mg

Ingredients:

- 1 lb ground lamb
- 1/2 cup breadcrumbs
- 1 egg, beaten
- 1 teaspoon ground cumin
- 1 teaspoon ground coriander
- 1/2 teaspoon cinnamon
- 1/4 teaspoon cayenne pepper
- 2 cloves garlic, minced
- Salt and pepper, to taste
- 2 tablespoons olive oil
- Fresh parsley and mint, chopped (for garnish)
- Yogurt, for serving

Step-by-Step Preparation:
1. In a bowl, combine lamb, breadcrumbs, egg, spices, garlic, salt, and pepper. Mix until well incorporated.
2. Form the mixture into small meatballs.
3. Heat olive oil in a skillet over medium heat. Add meatballs and cook until browned and cooked through.
4. Garnish with chopped parsley and mint. Serve warm with yogurt on the side.

Storage Guidelines:
- Once the lamb meatballs have cooled to room temperature, transfer them into an airtight container.
- Store the container in the refrigerator.
- The meatballs can be safely stored for up to 3-4 days.

Reheating Guidelines:
- **Oven Method (Preferred):**
1. Preheat your oven to 375°F (190°C).
2. Place the meatballs on an oven-safe dish or tray, ensuring they are spread out evenly.
3. Heat the meatballs for approximately 10-15 minutes or until they are warmed through.

- **Microwave Method:**
1. Place a portion of the meatballs on a microwave-safe plate.
2. Cover with a microwave-safe lid or plastic wrap, leaving a small vent for steam to escape.
3. Microwave on medium power for 1-2 minutes. Check to ensure they're heated through. If not, continue to microwave in additional 30-second intervals until warm.

Serving Suggestion:
- After reheating, it's best to garnish with fresh parsley and mint for added freshness.
- Serve with a dollop of yogurt on the side or drizzled on top.

Relish the exotic and flavorful experience of your reheated Moroccan Spiced Lamb Meatballs!

Embark on a delightful culinary adventure with Moroccan Spiced Lamb Meatballs. With each bite, experience a burst of exotic spices and high-quality protein that supports your muscle-building goals, making your dinner both flavorful and beneficial for your fitness journey.

33. Grilled Tuna with Mango Salsa

Discover the exquisite taste of Grilled Tuna Steak Slices with Mango Salsa and Vegetable Salad, a delightful pairing of protein-rich tuna and refreshing, fruity salsa. This dish is not only a treat for the taste buds but also a powerhouse of nutrients that support muscle gain.

Serving: 4
Prepping Time: 20 mins
Cook Time: 10 mins
Difficulty: Easy

Nutritional Facts (Per serving):
- Calories: 350
- Protein: 40g
- Carbohydrates: 20g
- Dietary Fiber: 3g
- Sugars: 16g
- Fat: 10g
- Saturated Fat: 2g
- Cholesterol: 65mg
- Sodium: 60mg

Ingredients:

- 4 tuna steaks
- Olive oil for brushing
- Salt and pepper, to taste
- 1 ripe mango, diced
- 1/2 red onion, finely chopped
- 1 jalapeno, minced
- Juice of 1 lime
- 2 tablespoons chopped cilantro
- Mixed salad greens

Step-by-Step Preparation:

1. Preheat the grill over medium-high heat.
2. Brush tuna steaks with olive oil and season with salt and pepper.
3. Grill for 1-2 minutes per side for medium-rare.
4. For the salsa, combine mango, red onion, jalapeno, lime juice, and cilantro in a bowl.
5. Serve grilled tuna over mixed salad greens and top with mango salsa.

Storage Guidelines:

- **Tuna Steak:** Once the grilled tuna has cooled to room temperature, transfer it to an airtight container.
- **Mango Salsa:** Store the salsa separately in a different airtight container to maintain its freshness.
- Both the tuna and the salsa should be refrigerated and consumed within 2 days for the best quality.

Reheating Guidelines:

- **Oven Method (Preferred):**
1. Preheat your oven to 325°F (165°C).
2. Place the tuna steaks on a baking sheet lined with aluminum foil.
3. Heat for approximately 5-7 minutes, ensuring you don't overcook, as tuna can dry out quickly.

- **Microwave Method:**
1. Place the tuna on a microwave-safe plate.
2. Heat on medium power for 1-2 minutes. Make sure to check after the first minute to avoid overcooking.

Note: Ideally, grilled tuna is best enjoyed freshly made, as reheating can alter its texture and taste.

- **Mango Salsa:**

Do not reheat the mango salsa. Simply remove it from the refrigerator and let it sit for 10-15 minutes to bring it to room temperature.

Serving Suggestion:

- After reheating the tuna, place it over fresh salad greens and top with the mango salsa for a refreshing meal.

Enjoy the combination of flavors and textures from the tender grilled tuna and the zesty mango salsa, making your meal both delicious and nutritionally balanced!

Dive into a plate of Grilled Tuna Steak with Mango Salsa for a refreshing yet protein-rich dining experience. The harmonious blend of savory tuna and sweet mango not only delights the palate but also fuels your muscle-building efforts with its high protein content.

34. Stir-Fried Beef with Mushrooms and Bell Peppers

Savor the delightful Stir-Fried Beef with Mushrooms and Bell Peppers, a vibrant, nutrient-dense dish that promises a burst of flavor. This protein-rich concoction is ideal for those on a muscle gain journey, offering a satisfying, wholesome dinner that pleases both the eye and palate.

Nutritional Facts (Per serving):
- Calories: 320
- Protein: 29g
- Carbohydrates: 11g
- Dietary Fiber: 2g
- Sugars: 4g
- Fat: 18g
- Saturated Fat: 5g
- Cholesterol: 70mg
- Sodium: 670mg

Ingredients:
- 1 lb beef sirloin, thinly sliced
- 2 tablespoons soy sauce
- 1 tablespoon oyster sauce
- 1 tablespoon cornstarch
- 2 tablespoons vegetable oil
- 1 cup mushrooms, sliced
- 1/2 green bell pepper, sliced
- 1/2 red bell pepper, sliced
- 2 cloves garlic, minced
- 1 teaspoon ginger, minced
- Green onions and sesame seeds for garnish

Step-by-Step Preparation:
1. Marinate beef with soy sauce, oyster sauce, and cornstarch in a bowl.
2. Heat oil in a wok or large skillet over medium-high heat.
3. Add beef and stir-fry until browned, then remove and set aside.
4. In the same wok, stir-fry garlic, ginger, mushrooms, and bell peppers until tender.
5. Return beef to the wok, mixing well. Garnish with green onions and sesame seeds.

Storage Guidelines:
- **Storing Leftovers:** Allow the stir-fried beef to cool to room temperature.
- **Airtight Container:** Place the cooled leftovers in an airtight container to prevent them from drying out and absorbing odors from the refrigerator.
- **Refrigeration:** Store the container in the refrigerator. The dish should be eaten within 1 to 2 days for optimal freshness and taste.

Reheating Guidelines:
- **Stovetop Method (Recommended):**
1. Heat a wok or skillet over medium heat.
2. Once hot, add the leftover stir-fried beef with mushrooms and bell peppers.
3. Stir frequently to distribute heat evenly.
4. Cook until the dish is heated through, which should take around 3-5 minutes. Avoid overcooking as the beef may become tough.

- **Microwave Method:**
1. Place a portion of the leftovers in a microwave-safe dish.
2. Cover with a microwave-safe lid or plastic wrap, leaving a small corner open to allow steam to escape.
3. Heat on medium power for 1-2 minutes, stirring halfway through to ensure even heating.
4. Be cautious of overcooking when using the microwave.

Serving Suggestion:
- Once reheated, give the dish a quick taste. Adjust the seasonings if necessary, as flavors might change slightly after storage.
- Before serving, add freshly chopped green onions and a sprinkle of sesame seeds for garnish.

Note: It's not advisable to freeze this dish as the beef and vegetables' textures may be adversely affected upon thawing and reheating.

Enjoy your reheated Stir-Fried Beef with Mushrooms and Bell Peppers with its retained flavors and textures, making your meal delightful and nutritionally balanced!

The Stir-Fried Beef with Mushrooms and Bell Peppers is not just a visual feast but a protein powerhouse that supports muscle gain. Each serving delivers delightful textures and flavors, ensuring a dinner experience that's as enjoyable as it is nourishing.

35. Lemon Herb Grilled Tilapia

Dive into a light yet protein-rich dish with Lemon Herb Grilled Tilapia. This straightforward, delightful recipe boasts a combination of fresh herbs and citrus flavors, making it a perfect, nutritious option for those working on muscle gain while seeking a meal that's easy on the palate.

Serving: 4
Prepping Time: 10 mins
Cook Time: 10 mins
Difficulty: Easy

Nutritional Facts (Per serving):
- Calories: 200
- Carbohydrates: 1g
- Sugars: 0g
- Saturated Fat: 2g
- Sodium: 60mg
- Protein: 23g
- Dietary Fiber: 0g
- Fat: 12g
- Cholesterol: 55mg

Ingredients:
- 4 tilapia fillets
- 2 tablespoons olive oil
- Juice of 1 lemon
- 1 teaspoon dried thyme
- 1 teaspoon dried rosemary
- 1 teaspoon garlic powder
- Salt and pepper, to taste
- Lemon wedges and fresh parsley for garnish

Step-by-Step Preparation:
1. Preheat the grill to medium-high heat.
2. Whisk together olive oil, lemon juice, thyme, rosemary, garlic powder, salt, and pepper in a bowl.
3. Brush tilapia fillets with the herb mixture.
4. Place fillets on the grill and cook for 4-5 minutes per side or until fish flakes easily.
5. Garnish with lemon wedges and fresh parsley before serving.

Storage Guidelines:
- **Cooling Before Storage:** Ensure the grilled tilapia has cooled to room temperature after cooking.
- **Airtight Containers:** Place each tilapia fillet in an airtight container. If stacking fillets, use parchment paper in between to prevent sticking.
- **Refrigeration:** Refrigerate the airtight container. Consuming the grilled tilapia within 1-2 days is best for optimal flavor and texture.

Reheating Guidelines:
- **Oven Method (Recommended):**
1. Preheat the oven to 350°F (175°C).
2. Place the tilapia fillets on a baking sheet lined with parchment paper or aluminum foil.
3. Bake for 8-10 minutes or until the fish is heated through. It's essential to cook enough to retain the fish's moisture.

- **Microwave Method:**
1. Place the tilapia fillets on a microwave-safe dish.
2. Heat on a medium setting for 1-2 minutes. Check the center of the fillet to ensure it's warmed through.
3. As microwaves may heat unevenly, be cautious not to overheat, as this can dry out the fish.

Note:
- Grilled tilapia is best enjoyed fresh, but if you must store leftovers, ensure they are reheated only once to maintain quality.
- It is not recommended to freeze the cooked tilapia as it may affect the texture and moisture content upon thawing and reheating.

Serving Suggestion:
- After reheating, serve the tilapia immediately for the best texture and flavor.
- You can add a fresh squeeze of lemon juice or a drizzle of olive oil on top for added moisture and flavor.

Enjoy your reheated Lemon Herb Grilled Tilapia, ensuring that it remains flavorful and retains its delicate texture, complementing your muscle-building journey with a delightful meal!

Lemon Herb Grilled Tilapia offers a simple, refreshing, yet protein-dense option for dinner, providing the essential nutrients needed for muscle building without compromising on taste. Its light, zesty flavors are perfect for a pleasant dining experience that supports your health and fitness goals.

36. Thai Green Curry with Chicken

Indulge in the exotic and flavorful Thai Green Curry with Chicken, a perfect fusion of creamy coconut milk, spicy green chilies, fresh basil, nutritious vegetables, and aromatic spices. This dish is not only a feast for the taste buds but also a protein-rich meal that supports your muscle-building goals.

Serving: 4
Prepping Time: 20 mins
Cook Time: 30 mins
Difficulty: Moderate

Nutritional Facts (Per serving):

- Calories: 420
- Carbohydrates: 18g
- Carbohydrates: 18g
- Saturated Fat: 20g
- Sodium: 720mg
- Protein: 28g
- Dietary Fiber: 2g
- Dietary Fiber: 2g
- Cholesterol: 70mg

Ingredients:

- 1 lb chicken breast, sliced
- 2 tablespoons green curry paste
- 1 can (14 oz) coconut milk
- 1 cup mixed vegetables (bell peppers, baby corn, etc.)
- 1/2 cup Thai basil leaves
- 2 green chilies, sliced
- 1 tablespoon fish sauce
- 1 tablespoon sugar
- 2 tablespoons vegetable oil
- Steamed rice for serving

Step-by-Step Preparation:

1. Heat oil in a pot over medium heat and sauté curry paste until aromatic.
2. Add chicken, cooking until it's browned.
3. Pour in coconut milk, bringing it to a simmer.
4. Introduce vegetables, fish sauce, and sugar, cooking until the vegetables are tender.
5. Finally, add basil and green chilies, cooking for an additional 2 minutes. Serve over steamed rice.

Storage Guidelines:
- **Cooling Before Storage:** Allow the Thai green curry to cool to room temperature after cooking.
- **Airtight Containers:** Transfer the cooled curry into an airtight container.
- **Refrigeration:** Store the container in the refrigerator. The curry will remain fresh and flavorful for up to 3 days.

Reheating Guidelines:
- **Stovetop Method (Recommended):**
1. Pour the curry into a saucepan.
2. Warm it over medium heat, stirring occasionally to ensure even heating.
3. Cook until it reaches a gentle simmer, ensuring the chicken is heated through.

- **Microwave Method:**
1. Transfer the desired amount of curry to a microwave-safe dish.
2. Cover the dish with a microwave-safe lid or wrap.
3. Heat on a medium setting for 2-3 minutes, stirring halfway to ensure even heating.
4. Ensure the chicken is thoroughly warm before consuming.

Note:
- Avoid frequent reheating, as this may affect the texture and flavor of the curry. Reheat only the amount you intend to consume.
- Add a few fresh basil leaves during the reheating process for optimal taste.

Serving Suggestion:
- After reheating, serve the Thai Green Curry with Chicken over freshly steamed rice for the best experience.
- A squeeze of fresh lime or a sprinkle of chopped cilantro can enhance the flavor.

Relish your Thai Green Curry with Chicken, ensuring its rich flavors and textures remain intact even after storage and reheating. This delicious dish promises a delightful culinary experience while aiding your muscle-building journey.

Embark on a culinary adventure with Thai Green Curry with Chicken, a dish that's as nutritious as it is flavorful. Every serving promises a protein boost to aid in muscle building, along with a delightful array of tastes and textures to satisfy your palate.

Note:

★★★★★ **Leave a Review** ★★★★★

As an independent author with a small marketing budget, reviews are my livelihood on this platform. If you enjoyed this book, I'd appreciate it if you could leave your honest feedback. I read EVERY single review because I love the feedback from MY readers!

If you do not know what to write, you can simply choose a star rating (one to five stars), which only takes a moment.

Thank you in advance for leaving a rating or review. We appreciate you!

1. **FIND** this book on Amazon
2. **SCROLL** down to the reviews
3. **SELECT**

Write a customer review

Contents

Recipe 37: **Spicy Tuna Stuffed Avocado Halves** 90

Recipe 38: **Roasted Red Pepper Hummus** 92

Recipe 39: **Baked Kale Chips With Parmesan** 94

Recipe 40: **High-Protein Trail Mix With Nuts and Seeds** 96

Recipe 41: **Greek Yogurt and Dill Dip** 98

Recipe 42: **Cottage Cheese and Pineapple Bowl** 100

Recipe 43: **Asparagus and Mushrooms Sauteed With Lemon Zest** .. 102

Recipe 44: **Protein-Packed Guacamole With Hemp Seeds** 104

Recipe 45: **Quinoa Tabbouleh Salad** 106

Recipe 46: **Peanut Butter and Oatmeal Protein Energy Balls** 108

Recipe 47: **Protein Boost Spicy Roasted Chickpeas** 110

Recipe 48: **Tofu and Veggie Spring Rolls** 112

Chapter 6: Protein-Infused Snacks & Sides: For Muscle Gain

37. Spicy Tuna Stuffed Avocado Halves

Indulge in the vibrant, tasty, Spicy Tuna Stuffed Avocado Halves with Red Onion and Celery Salad. This nutritious snack is a delightful union of spicy tuna and creamy avocado, accompanied by a crunchy, zesty salad, offering a protein boost essential for muscle building while thrilling your taste buds.

Serving: 2
Prepping Time: 15 mins
Cook Time: 0 mins
Difficulty: Easy

Nutritional Facts (Per serving):
- Calories: 310
- Carbohydrates: 12g
- Sugars: 3g
- Saturated Fat: 3.5g
- Sodium: 460mg
- Protein: 20g
- Dietary Fiber: 8g
- Fat: 22g
- Cholesterol: 35mg

Ingredients:
- 1 ripe avocado, halved and pitted
- 1 can (5 oz) tuna, drained
- 1 tablespoon mayonnaise
- 1 teaspoon Sriracha
- 1 teaspoon soy sauce
- 1/2 red onion, finely chopped
- 1 celery stalk, finely chopped
- 1 teaspoon sesame oil
- 1 teaspoon sesame seeds
- Fresh cilantro for garnish

Step-by-Step Preparation:
1. Combine tuna, mayonnaise, Sriracha, soy sauce, red onion, celery, and sesame oil in a bowl.
2. Mix thoroughly until the ingredients are well incorporated.
3. Carefully spoon the spicy tuna mixture into the avocado halves.
4. Garnish with sesame seeds and fresh cilantro.

Storage Guidelines:
- **Immediate Storage:** As both avocado and tuna can change texture and flavor upon storage, this dish is best enjoyed fresh. If necessary, store in the refrigerator for a few hours before serving.
- **Avoid Long-Term Storage:** This recipe isn't ideal for long-term storage as the avocado tends to brown, and the freshness of the tuna mixture will decline.
- **Airtight Container:** If you must store it, place the stuffed avocados in an airtight container to minimize exposure to air.

Short-Term Refrigeration (if necessary):
- Store for no more than 1-2 hours in the refrigerator before consumption to maintain the best texture and flavor.

Reheating Guidelines:
- **No Reheating Necessary:** This dish is served cold and does not require reheating. If stored in the refrigerator, remove it and let it sit for a few minutes at room temperature before serving.

Note:
- Consider preparing and consuming this dish fresh each time for optimal taste rather than storing it.
- If you're prepping ahead, you can keep the tuna mixture stored separately in the fridge and assemble it with fresh avocado when ready to serve.

Serving Suggestion:
- For added zest and flavor, consider adding a squeeze of fresh lime or lemon juice over the top before serving.
- Indulge in the Spicy Tuna Stuffed Avocado Halves responsibly. Remember that this delicacy is best savored fresh to ensure you experience its full array of delightful textures and flavors while gaining the protein necessary for building muscle.

Relish in the flavorful and nutritious Spicy Tuna Stuffed Avocado Halves with Red Onion and Celery Salad, a snack designed for those building muscle. With its high protein content and an array of delightful flavors, it's not only a healthy but utterly satisfying snack for your fitness journey.

38. Roasted Red Pepper Hummus

Dive into the rich and smooth Roasted Red Pepper Hummus with Pita Chips, a snack that's not only bursting with delightful flavors but also packed with protein. The smoky sweetness of roasted red peppers blended into creamy hummus makes for a tempting treat that supports your muscle-building efforts.

Serving: 6
Prepping Time: 10 mins
Cook Time: 0 mins
Difficulty: Easy

Nutritional Facts (Per serving):
- Calories: 210
- Protein: 7g
- Carbohydrates: 30g
- Dietary Fiber: 5g
- Sugars: 2g
- Fat: 8g
- Saturated Fat: 1g
- Cholesterol: 0mg
- Sodium: 310mg

Ingredients:
- 2 cups canned chickpeas, rinsed and drained
- 1 cup roasted red peppers
- 2 cloves garlic, minced
- 3 tablespoons tahini
- 2 tablespoons olive oil
- 2 tablespoons lemon juice
- 1 teaspoon ground cumin
- Salt, to taste
- 6 pita bread, cut into wedges

Step-by-Step Preparation:
1. Combine chickpeas, roasted red peppers, garlic, tahini, olive oil, lemon juice, cumin, and salt in a food processor.
2. Blend until smooth and creamy.
3. Adjust seasoning if necessary and serve with pita chips.

Storage Guidelines:
- **Refrigeration:** Store the hummus in an airtight container in the refrigerator. It should stay fresh for up to one week.
- **Separate Storage:** Store pita chips separately in a sealed bag or container at room temperature to maintain their crispness.
- **Avoid Freezing:** Freezing is not recommended, as it may alter the consistency and flavor of the hummus.

Reheating Guidelines:
- **No Reheating Necessary for Hummus:** Hummus is typically served cold or at room temperature. Remove it from the refrigerator and let it sit out briefly to reach room temperature before serving.
- **Reheating Pita Chips (if necessary):** If the pita chips lose their crispness, reheat them in the oven. Preheat the oven to 375°F (190°C), spread the chips on a baking sheet, and bake for approximately 5 minutes or until crispy.

Serving Suggestion:
- Before serving, try to drizzle olive oil over the hummus and garnish with a sprinkle of paprika or chopped fresh parsley for added flavor and presentation.
- Hummus can also be served with fresh vegetable sticks (like carrot, cucumber, or bell pepper) for a gluten-free option.
- With the Roasted Red Pepper Hummus, you have a tasty, protein-rich snack that is pleasing to the palate and beneficial for muscle-building efforts. Always consider making it fresh to savor its full flavor and nutritional value.

With Roasted Red Pepper Hummus with Pita Chips, snacking transforms into an enjoyable and healthful experience. This delightful dish, rich in proteins, aids muscle-building while delivering a burst of vibrant, satisfying flavors, making it a favorite for those on their journey to fitness.

39. Baked Kale Chips With Parmesan

Unveil the joy of guilt-free snacking with Baked Kale Chips with Parmesan. These crispy, savory chips not only satiate your taste buds but also provide a protein punch, serving as an ideal snack for those engaged in muscle-building workouts while keeping the calorie count in check.

Serving: 4
Prepping Time: 10 mins
Cook Time: 20 mins
Difficulty: Easy

Nutritional Facts (Per serving):
- Calories: 120
- Protein: 6g
- Carbohydrates: 10g
- Dietary Fiber: 2g
- Sugars: 0g
- Fat: 7g
- Saturated Fat: 2g
- Cholesterol: 7mg
- Sodium: 220mg

Ingredients:

- 1 bunch of kale, washed and dried
- 1 tablespoon olive oil
- 1/4 cup grated Parmesan cheese
- 1/2 teaspoon garlic powder
- Salt and black pepper to taste

Step-by-Step Preparation:

1. Preheat oven to 350°F (175°C).
2. Remove kale stems and tear them into bite-size pieces.
3. In a bowl, toss kale with olive oil, Parmesan, garlic powder, salt, and pepper.
4. Arrange kale in a single layer on a baking sheet.
5. Bake until crispy, being cautious not to burn.

Storage Guidelines:
- **Room Temperature:** Store the baked kale chips in an airtight container or zip-top bag at room temperature. They should retain their crispiness for 2-3 days.
- **Avoid Moisture:** Ensure the kale chips are completely cooled before storing them to prevent any moisture, which can make them soggy.
- **Refrigeration:** It's best not to refrigerate kale chips as the humidity can soften them.

Reheating Guidelines:
- **Oven Method:** If your kale chips lose their crispiness, you can restore them by preheating your oven to 300°F (150°C). Place the chips in a single layer on a baking sheet and reheat for about 3-5 minutes. Be sure to monitor them closely to avoid burning.

Serving Suggestion:
- Kale chips are best enjoyed immediately after baking to maintain their crunch.
- They can be paired with a dipping sauce or enjoyed independently for a light, crunchy snack.

Baked Kale Chips with Parmesan offer a delicious, protein-rich alternative to traditional chips. They're perfect for satisfying savory cravings while supporting your muscle-building goals. Remember to enjoy them soon after baking to relish their crispy texture and flavor.

End your cravings with the crunchy, savory delight of Baked Kale Chips with Parmesan. This snack is not only delectable but also a protein-rich ally in your muscle-gaining journey, making each bite not only satisfying but also beneficial for your fitness objectives.

40. High-Protein Trail Mix With Nuts and Seeds

Discover the energizing High-Protein Trail Mix with Nuts and Seeds, a delightful blend of crunchy nuts and sweet dried fruits. This power-packed snack offers a quick protein boost, essential for muscle gain, making it an ideal pick-me-up for fitness enthusiasts and individuals on the go.

- Serving: 10
- Prepping Time: 10 mins
- Cook Time: 0 mins
- Difficulty: Easy

Nutritional Facts (Per serving):

- Calories: 300
- Carbohydrates: 20g
- Sugars: 10g
- Saturated Fat: 2.5g
- Sodium: 20mg
- Protein: 10g
- Dietary Fiber: 5g
- Fat: 23g
- Cholesterol: 0mg

Ingredients:

- 1 cup walnuts
- 1 cup almonds
- 1/2 cup peanuts
- 1/2 cup raisins
- 1/2 cup sultanas
- 1/2 cup pumpkin seeds
- 1/2 cup sunflower seeds
- 1/4 cup chia seeds
- Pinch of salt

Step-by-Step Preparation:

1. Combine all nuts, dried fruits, and seeds in a large mixing bowl.
2. Add a pinch of salt and toss the mixture until well combined.
3. Store in an airtight container and keep in a cool, dry place.

Storage Guidelines:
- **Airtight Container:** Store the trail mix in an airtight container to maintain the freshness and crunchiness of the nuts and seeds.
- **Cool, Dry Place:** Keep the container in a cool, dry place, away from direct sunlight. The pantry or a kitchen cupboard is ideal.
- **Longevity:** The trail mix should stay fresh for up to 2 months when stored properly.
- **Avoid Moisture:** Ensure the container is sealed tightly to prevent moisture, which can spoil the nuts and dried fruits.

Reheating Guidelines:
- **Not Necessary:** This trail mix is meant to be consumed at room temperature and does not require reheating. Reheating may cause the dried fruits to harden and the nuts to over-roast, altering their flavors and textures.

Serving Suggestion:
- This trail mix is ready to eat straight from the container.
- It makes for a convenient and healthy snack on the go, ideal for pre-or post-workout, hiking, or as a midday energy booster.
- You can also sprinkle it over yogurt or incorporate it into your breakfast cereal for added flavor and nutrition.

High-Protein Trail Mix With Nuts and Seeds is a practical and nutritious snack for those needing an energy and protein boost during the day. Its mix of flavors and textures from the various nuts, seeds, and dried fruits offers a satisfying and enjoyable eating experience while supporting your muscle-building efforts.

The High-Protein Trail Mix with Nuts and Seeds is not only a tasty snack but a powerhouse of energy and protein. Its careful blend of ingredients supports muscle gain while offering a satisfying, on-the-go snack that fuels your active lifestyle with delightful flavors and essential nutrients.

41. Greek Yogurt and Dill Dip

Dive into a traditional Mediterranean delight with the Greek Yogurt and Dill Dip inspired by the **classic Tzatziki**. A perfect fusion of creamy yogurt, crisp cucumber, aromatic dill, and spicy garlic, this dip is not only a treat to the taste buds but also a protein powerhouse aiding in muscle gain.

- Serving: 6
- Prepping Time: 15 mins
- Cook Time: 0 mins
- Difficulty: Easy

Nutritional Facts (Per serving):
- Calories: 80
- Carbohydrates: 5g
- Sugars: 4g
- Saturated Fat: 0.5g
- Sodium: 200mg
- Protein: 7g
- Dietary Fiber: 0g
- Fat: 3.5g
- Cholesterol: 6mg

Ingredients:

- 2 cups Greek yogurt
- 1/2 cucumber, finely grated and drained
- 3 tablespoons fresh dill, chopped
- 2 cloves garlic, minced
- 1 tablespoon olive oil
- 1 teaspoon salt, or to taste
- 1 tablespoon lemon juice

Step-by-Step Preparation:

1. In a bowl, combine Greek yogurt, grated cucumber, dill, minced garlic, and lemon juice.
2. Season with salt and mix until well combined.
3. Drizzle with olive oil and give it a final stir.
4. Refrigerate for at least 2 hours before serving to let the flavors meld.

Storage Guidelines:
- **Refrigeration:** Always store the dip in the refrigerator as it contains dairy.
- **Airtight Container:** Place the dip in an airtight container to maintain its freshness and prevent it from absorbing odors from other foods in the refrigerator.
- **Shelf Life:** When stored properly, the dip will remain fresh for 3-4 days.
- **Check Consistency:** Before using it after storage, stir the dip quickly. If any excess liquid forms at the top (from the yogurt or cucumbers), you can either stir it in or pour it off.

Reheating Guidelines:
- **Not Recommended:** This dip is designed to be consumed cold. Reheating may affect its texture and taste, making it less appealing.

Serving Suggestion:
- Take the dip out of the refrigerator for about 10 minutes before serving to temper its chill a bit.
- For a healthy snack, serve with fresh vegetable sticks like carrots, celery, or bell peppers.
- It can also be served alongside grilled meats or used as a spread for sandwiches or wraps.
- For an authentic experience, serve with pita bread or pita chips.

The Greek Yogurt and Dill Dip is a refreshing and nutritious choice for any snack or appetizer spread. Its blend of flavors and creamy texture makes it a favorite, while its high protein content supports your muscle-building and overall health goals.

Embrace the rich flavors of the Mediterranean with the Greek Yogurt and Dill Dip. This snack is not just about a delightful taste; its high protein content ensures you're fueling your muscles right. Perfect for dipping veggies or spreading on whole-grain bread, it's a wholesome choice for those serious about muscle gain and taste alike.

42. Cottage Cheese and Pineapple Bowl

Energize your day with a Cottage Cheese and Pineapple Bowl, combining the creaminess of cottage cheese with the tangy sweetness of pineapple. This delightful, protein-rich bowl promotes muscle gain while offering a refreshing and tasty snack or side dish that is sure to satisfy your cravings.

Serving: 4
Prepping Time: 10 mins
Cook Time: 0 mins
Difficulty: Easy

Nutritional Facts (Per serving):
- Calories: 210
- Carbohydrates: 18g
- Sugars: 15g
- Saturated Fat: 1g
- Sodium: 400mg
- Protein: 28g
- Dietary Fiber: 1g
- Fat: 2g
- Cholesterol: 5mg

Ingredients:
- 2 cups cottage cheese
- 1 cup fresh pineapple chunks
- 1 tablespoon honey
- 1/4 teaspoon vanilla extract
- 2 tablespoons shredded coconut
- 1 tablespoon chopped nuts (optional)

Step-by-Step Preparation:
1. In individual bowls, place equal portions of cottage cheese.
2. Top with fresh pineapple chunks.
3. Drizzle honey and vanilla extract over each serving.
4. Sprinkle with shredded coconut and chopped nuts if desired.
5. Serve immediately or refrigerate until ready to serve.

Storage Guidelines:
- **Refrigeration:** Since the dish contains dairy, it should be stored in the refrigerator.
- **Airtight Container:** Use an airtight container to prevent the cottage cheese from absorbing odors and to keep the pineapple fresh.
- **Separate Storage:** For optimal freshness, consider storing the cottage cheese and pineapple separately and combining them before serving.
- **Shelf Life:** The prepared dish should be consumed within 1-2 days for the best flavor and texture.

No Reheating Necessary:
- **Cold Dish:** This dish is meant to be enjoyed cold, and reheating is not recommended. Reheating cottage cheese can alter its texture and flavor, and the pineapple may become mushy.

Serving Suggestions After Storage:
- If stored separately, combine the cottage cheese and pineapple, then add the honey, vanilla, coconut, and nuts (if using) just before serving.
- Give the dish a gentle stir to incorporate any settled juices or honey.
- Consider adding a fresh drizzle of honey or a sprinkle of coconut on top for added flavor and presentation.

The Cottage Cheese and Pineapple Bowl is a delightful and nutritious option, perfect for a snack or light breakfast. Its creamy and tangy-sweet flavors are satisfying, while the high protein content supports your muscle-building goals. Enjoy it fresh for the best experience!

Relish the delightful combo of Cottage Cheese and Pineapple Bowl, a quick and easy snack that supports your muscle-building goals. Its high protein content, coupled with the refreshing taste of pineapple and the sweetness of honey, makes it a delightful, guilt-free treat for any time of the day.

43. Asparagus and Mushrooms Sauteed With Lemon Zest

Revitalize your snack time with Asparagus and Mushrooms Sautéed With Lemon Zest, a vibrant and irresistible side dish that is as nutritious as it is flavorful. It's a protein-enriched choice that supports muscle gain while tantalizing your taste buds.

Serving: 4
Prepping Time: 10 mins
Cook Time: 12 mins
Difficulty: Easy

Nutritional Facts (Per serving):

- Calories: 70
- Carbohydrates: 6g
- Sugars: 3g
- Saturated Fat: 1g
- Sodium: 5mg
- Protein: 3g
- Dietary Fiber: 2g
- Fat: 5g
- Cholesterol: 0mg

Ingredients:

- 1 bunch asparagus, trimmed and cut
- 1 cup mushrooms, sliced
- 1 tablespoon olive oil
- 1 teaspoon lemon zest
- Salt and pepper to taste
- 1 tablespoon fresh parsley, chopped (optional)

Step-by-Step Preparation:

1. Heat olive oil in a skillet over medium heat.
2. Add asparagus and mushrooms, sautéing until tender and slightly brown.
3. Season with salt and pepper to taste.
4. Just before removing from heat, add lemon zest and stir well.
5. Garnish with chopped parsley if desired before serving.

Storage Guidelines:
- **Refrigeration:** Store the cooled leftovers in an airtight container in the refrigerator.
- **Shelf Life:** The sautéed asparagus and mushrooms are best enjoyed within 1-2 days of storage to maintain their flavor and texture.

Reheating:
- **Stovetop Method:** Reheat the dish in a skillet over medium heat. Add a small amount of olive oil or butter to prevent sticking, and rehydrate the vegetables. Stir occasionally until warmed through. Avoid overcooking to prevent the vegetables from becoming mushy.
- **Microwave Method:** Place the leftovers in a microwave-safe dish, covering it loosely. Heat on medium power in 30-second increments, stirring between each, until warmed. Be cautious not to overheat as the vegetables can lose their crispness.

Additional Tips:
- Consider adding a fresh sprinkle of lemon zest or a squeeze of lemon juice to revive the dish's citrus notes when reheating.
- If the dish appears dry upon reheating, a drizzle of olive oil can restore moisture without making the vegetables soggy.
- For an extra layer of flavor, consider garnishing with freshly chopped herbs like parsley or chives before serving.

Remember, the key to enjoying leftover sautéed vegetables is storing and heating them carefully to preserve their natural textures and flavors. The Asparagus and Mushrooms Sautéed with Lemon Zest is a nutritious and delightful dish that can be quickly revived for a second serving!

Add a burst of flavor and nutrition to your day with Asparagus and Mushrooms Sautéed With Lemon Zest. This quick and simple dish offers a protein boost to support muscle gain, all while delighting your palate with its fresh and zesty taste profile. Perfect for a midday snack or a dinner side!

44. Protein-Packed Guacamole With Hemp Seeds

Indulge guilt-free with the Protein-Packed Guacamole with Hemp Seeds, a tasty snack filled with healthy fats and protein. This delicious and easy-to-make dish is perfect for muscle gain and overall wellness.

Serving: 4
Prepping Time: 15 mins
Cook Time: 0 mins
Difficulty: Easy

Nutritional Facts (Per serving):
- Calories: 240
- Carbohydrates: 15g
- Sugars: 2g
- Saturated Fat: 3g
- Sodium: 300mg
- Protein: 7g
- Dietary Fiber: 11g
- Fat: 20g
- Cholesterol: 0mg

Ingredients:
- 3 ripe avocados, peeled and pitted
- 3 tablespoons hemp seeds
- 1 small red onion, finely chopped
- Juice of 1 fresh lime
- 1/2 teaspoon pink sea salt
- 2 tablespoons fresh cilantro, chopped
- 1 medium tomato, diced
- 1 jalapeno, de-seeded and chopped (optional)

Step-by-Step Preparation:
1. Mash the avocados in a bowl until smooth.
2. Add hemp seeds, red onion, lime juice, sea salt, cilantro, tomato, and jalapeno. Mix well.
3. Adjust salt and lime juice to taste.
4. Serve immediately with your favorite chips or fresh veggies.

Storage Guidelines:
- **Refrigeration:** Place any leftover guacamole in an airtight container. To prevent browning, press a piece of plastic wrap directly against the surface of the guacamole before sealing the container.
- **Shelf Life:** Consume the stored guacamole within 1-2 days. Since avocados brown quickly upon exposure to air, it's best to enjoy the dish as soon as possible for optimal flavor and color.

Reheating:
- Guacamole is traditionally served cold or at room temperature. It's not recommended to reheat it, as heat can alter the flavor and texture of the avocado and other fresh ingredients.

Refreshing for Service:
- If the guacamole has browned slightly in storage, you may gently scrape off the top layer to reveal the greener dip underneath.
- Consider adding a fresh squeeze of lime juice on top to revive the flavors before serving.
- Adjust the salt and mix gently to incorporate any separated ingredients if needed.

Additional Tips:
- For more extended storage (though not ideal), consider freezing the guacamole. Note that while freezing might slightly alter the texture, the flavor should largely remain intact. To use, thaw it in the refrigerator and give it a good stir before serving.

By following these storage and serving instructions, you can extend the life of your Protein-Packed Guacamole With Hemp Seeds and maintain its delightful flavors. Whether enjoyed immediately or saved for later, this nutritious snack is a tasty addition to your muscle-building dietary regimen.

This Protein-Packed Guacamole with Hemp Seeds isn't just your ordinary dip — it's a nutritional powerhouse designed for muscle growth and retention. Its delightful taste and texture make it a favorite for any occasion. Enjoy the burst of flavors while building your best body!

45. Quinoa Tabbouleh Salad

Dive into the refreshing Tabbouleh Salad with Quinoa, a perfect blend of nutrients and flavors designed for a quick protein boost and muscle gain. This vibrant, delightful salad is your go-to health companion!

Serving: 4
Prepping Time: 20 mins
Cook Time: 0 mins
Difficulty: Easy

Nutritional Facts (Per serving):
- Calories: 180
- Protein: 5g
- Carbohydrates: 20g
- Dietary Fiber: 4g
- Sugars: 3g
- Fat: 10g
- Saturated Fat: 1.5g
- Cholesterol: 0mg
- Sodium: 80mg

Ingredients:

- 1 cup cooked quinoa
- 1 bunch fresh parsley, finely chopped
- 1/4 cup fresh mint, finely chopped
- 2 tomatoes, diced
- 1 cucumber, diced
- 1/4 cup extra virgin olive oil
- 3 tablespoons lemon juice
- Salt and pepper to taste

Step-by-Step Preparation:

1. Combine quinoa, parsley, mint, tomatoes, and cucumber in a large bowl.
2. Whisk together olive oil, lemon juice, salt, and pepper in a separate small bowl.
3. Pour the dressing over the salad and toss to combine.
4. Serve chilled or at room temperature.

Storage Guidelines:
- **Refrigeration:** Transfer any leftover Quinoa Tabbouleh Salad into an airtight container and store it in the refrigerator.
- **Shelf Life:** The salad is best consumed within 2-3 days for optimal freshness. Over time, the vegetables may release moisture, causing the salad to become a bit soggy.

Reheating:
- Quinoa Tabbouleh Salad is traditionally served chilled or at room temperature. It's not recommended to reheat it, as this can alter the texture of the fresh ingredients and diminish the salad's vibrant flavors.

Refreshing for Service:
- If the salad has settled or the ingredients have separated during storage, gently stir before serving.
- Consider adding a fresh splash of lemon juice or a drizzle of olive oil to revive the flavors before serving. Adjust seasoning with salt and pepper if needed.

Additional Tips:
- If you're storing the salad for future consumption, keep the dressing separate and mix it before serving. This step can help preserve the crispness of the vegetables.

Following these storage and serving recommendations ensures that your Quinoa Tabbouleh Salad remains fresh, delicious, and ready to enjoy anytime. This nutritious dish provides both a burst of Mediterranean flavors and the protein essential for muscle gain.

Refresh your palate with the delightful Tabbouleh Salad with Quinoa, Parsley, and Vegetables. This energizing and protein-packed dish not only supports muscle gain but also pleases your taste buds with its burst of fresh and savory flavors!

46. Peanut Butter and Oatmeal Protein Energy Balls

Enjoy a delightful fusion of flavors with the Peanut Butter and Oatmeal Energy Balls. These protein-packed treats not only support muscle growth but also satisfy your sweet cravings.

- Serving: 12 balls
- Prepping Time: 10 mins
- Cook Time: 0 mins
- Difficulty: Easy

Nutritional Facts (Per serving):
- Calories: 120
- Carbohydrates: 14g
- Sugars: 8g
- Saturated Fat: 2g
- Sodium: 40mg
- Protein: 4g
- Dietary Fiber: 2g
- Fat: 6g
- Cholesterol: 0mg

Ingredients:

- 1 cup old-fashioned oats
- 1/2 cup peanut butter
- 1/4 cup honey
- 1/2 cup mini chocolate chips
- 1 tsp vanilla extract
- A pinch of salt

Step-by-Step Preparation:

1. Combine oats, peanut butter, honey, chocolate chips, vanilla, and salt in a large bowl.
2. Mix until well combined.
3. Roll the mixture into 1-inch balls.
4. Place on a parchment-lined tray and refrigerate for at least 1 hour before serving.

Storage Guidelines:
- **Refrigeration:** Store the energy balls in an airtight container in the refrigerator. Placing parchment paper between layers of balls can prevent sticking.
- **Shelf Life:** They can be kept in the fridge for up to 1-2 weeks.
- **Freezing:** For more extended storage, consider freezing the balls. Place them on a baking sheet lined with parchment paper in the freezer until solid, then transfer to a zip-top freezer bag or airtight container. They can be stored in the freezer for up to 3 months.

Reheating:
- **No Reheating Required:** These energy balls are meant to be eaten chilled or at room temperature. Remove them from the refrigerator or freezer and let them sit out for a few minutes before enjoying them. Do not reheat; this can cause the balls to lose shape and texture.

Serving from Freezer:
- If serving from the freezer, allow the balls to thaw at room temperature for about 10-15 minutes before eating for the best texture.

Additional Tips:
- You might serve them directly from the refrigerator or freezer for a firmer texture. For a softer, chewier bite, let them sit at room temperature for a little longer before serving.

By following these storage and serving tips, you can enjoy the delightful taste and protein benefits of the Peanut Butter and Oatmeal Protein Energy Balls anytime you need a tasty, energy-boosting snack.

These energy balls offer a harmonious blend of creamy peanut butter and chewy oats, heightened by sweet honey and chocolate chips. They're the perfect protein-packed treat for on-the-go snacking or a post-workout boost.

47. Protein Boost Spicy Roasted Chickpeas

Unleash the power of protein with these Spicy Roasted Chickpeas! Perfect as a snack or side, these crispy bites are not only filling but are also brimming with flavor and nutritional value to support muscle gain.

Serving: 4
Prepping Time: 10 mins
Cook Time: 20-25 mins
Difficulty: Easy

Nutritional Facts (Per serving):
- Calories: 200
- Protein: 10g
- Carbs: 30g
- Fat: 5g

Ingredients:

- 2 cans chickpeas, drained
- 1 tbsp olive oil
- 1 tsp chili powder
- 1 tsp garlic powder
- Salt to taste

Step-by-Step Preparation:

1. Preheat oven to 425°F.
2. Toss chickpeas in olive oil, chili powder, garlic powder, and salt.
3. Spread on a baking sheet in a single layer.
4. Roast for 20-25 minutes or until crispy.

Storage Guidelines:
- **Cooling:** Ensure the roasted chickpeas are completely cool before storing them. This step prevents them from becoming soggy.
- **Container:** Store the cooled chickpeas in an airtight container to maintain their crispness. Glass jars with tight-fitting lids work exceptionally well.
- **Shelf Life:** When stored in a cool, dry place, the chickpeas should maintain their crispness for 1 to 2 weeks.
- **Refrigeration:** It's not necessary to refrigerate the chickpeas, and doing so makes them lose their crispness more quickly.

Reheating:
- **Oven Reheating:** If the chickpeas lose their crispness, reheat them in the oven. Place them on a baking sheet in a single layer and bake at 400°F for 5 to 10 minutes or until they regain their crunch. Be careful not to over-bake, which can lead to overly rigid chickpeas.

Additional Tips:
- Avoid storing in humid places, as it can cause the chickpeas to become soggy.
- It's crucial not to store the chickpeas while they're still warm, as the trapped heat can create steam inside the container, leading to sogginess.

By adhering to these storage and reheating instructions, you can enjoy the crispy, flavorful Spicy Roasted Chickpeas while maintaining their original taste and texture, making them a delightful and convenient protein-rich snack.

This snack will become your go-to for a protein-packed crunch that's irresistibly tasty and supportive of your muscle-building goals. Perfect for on-the-go snacking or tossing into a salad for extra protein!

48. Tofu and Veggie Spring Rolls

Kick-start your muscle gain with these Tofu and Veggie Spring Rolls! A vibrant mix of tofu and fresh vegetables, paired with a protein-rich peanut sauce, offers a tasty, nutritious snack or side to complement your fitness journey.

Serving: 6
Prepping Time: 25 mins
Cook Time: None
Difficulty: Intermediate

Nutritional Facts (Per serving):
- Calories: 220
- Protein: 12g
- Carbs: 28g
- Fat: 8g

Ingredients:

- 12 rice paper wrappers
- 1 block extra-firm tofu, sliced thinly
- 2 carrots, julienned
- 1 cucumber, julienned
- 1 red bell pepper, sliced
- 1/2 cup fresh cilantro
- For Peanut Sauce:
  - 1/2 cup peanut butter
  - 2 tablespoons soy sauce
  - 1 tablespoon lime juice
  - 2 teaspoons honey
  - Water, as needed, to thin

Step-by-Step Preparation:

1. Prepare vegetables and tofu.
2. Soften rice paper in warm water.
3. Arrange tofu and veggies on rice paper, then roll tightly.
4. For sauce, whisk together all ingredients, adjusting consistency with water.
5. Serve rolls with peanut sauce for dipping.

Storage Guidelines:

<u>Spring Rolls:</u>

Short-Term Storage:
- Place the spring rolls in a container with a lid, but avoid stacking them directly on top of one another. If necessary, use parchment paper or plastic wrap to separate layers of spring rolls to prevent sticking.
- Ensure the container is airtight to maintain freshness.
- Store in the refrigerator if you plan to consume them within 1-2 days.

Not Suitable for Long-Term Storage:
- These spring rolls are best enjoyed fresh. They don't freeze well, as the rice paper might become soggy upon thawing.

<u>Peanut Sauce:</u>
- The peanut sauce can be stored in an airtight container in the refrigerator for up to a week.
- Stir well before each use, as separation may occur over time.

Reheating:

<u>Spring Rolls:</u>
- Spring rolls are typically enjoyed cold or at room temperature and do not need reheating.
- If refrigerated, consider taking them out a few minutes before consumption to allow them to come to room temperature for optimal flavor and texture.

<u>Peanut Sauce:</u>
- The peanut sauce can be served cold, or you may warm it gently for a more fluid consistency.
- To warm, heat the sauce in a small pot over low heat, stirring constantly to prevent burning. Alternatively, you can microwave the sauce in short intervals, stirring between each, until it reaches your desired temperature.

Additional Tips:
- The vegetables inside the rolls may release moisture over time, so the rolls are best consumed within a day for the best texture and flavor.

Following these storage and reheating guidelines, you can enjoy your Tofu and Veggie Spring Rolls with Peanut Dipping Sauce while preserving their fresh and delightful taste.

These spring rolls are flavorful and high in protein - a great choice for a quick and healthy snack! They're easy to carry, helping you stay energized and focused on building muscle.

Note:

★★★★★ **Leave a Review** ★★★★★

As an independent author with a small marketing budget, reviews are my livelihood on this platform. If you enjoyed this book, I'd appreciate it if you could leave your honest feedback. I read EVERY single review because I love the feedback from MY readers!

If you do not know what to write, you can simply choose a star rating (one to five stars), which only takes a moment.

Thank you in advance for leaving a rating or review. We appreciate you!

1. **FIND** this book on Amazon
2. **SCROLL** down to the reviews
3. **SELECT**

Write a customer review

Contents

Recipe 49: **Chocolate Avocado Protein Mousse with Pistachios** ... 116

Recipe 50: **Vanilla Protein Cheesecake with Berry Compote** 118

Recipe 51: **Mocha Chocolate Coffee Protein Smoothie** 120

Recipe 52: **Strawberry Protein Milkshake** 122

Recipe 53: **Chocolate Protein Brownies with Walnuts** 124

Recipe 54: **Chocolate Peanut Butter Protein Cookies** 126

Recipe 55: **Almond Joy Protein Shake** 128

Recipe 56: **Banana Nut Muffins** 130

Recipe 57: **Matcha Green Tea Smoothie With Berries Topping** 132

Recipe 58: **Banana Peanut Butter Protein Shake** 134

Recipe 59: **Coconut White Chocolate Protein Truffles** 136

Recipe 60: **Vanilla Protein Donuts with Chocolate Glaze** 138

Chapter 7: Muscle Building Indulgences: Desserts & Beverages

49. Chocolate Avocado Protein Mousse with Pistachios

Dive into Chocolate Avocado Protein Mousse's creamy, luscious texture with Pistachios, where indulgence meets nutrition. This silky, rich mousse combines the goodness of avocados, the power of protein, and the crunch of pistachios, making it a delightful and healthy treat for everyone.

- Serving: 4
- Prepping Time: 15 mins
- Cook Time: 0 mins (requires chilling)
- Difficulty: Easy

Nutritional Facts (Per serving):
- Calories: 280
- Protein: 10g
- Fat: 18g
- Carbohydrates: 25g

Ingredients:
- 2 ripe avocados
- 1/4 cup unsweetened cocoa powder
- 1/4 cup vanilla protein powder
- 1/4 cup honey or agave syrup
- 1 teaspoon vanilla extract
- Pinch of sea salt
- 1/4 cup chopped pistachios for garnish

Step-by-Step Preparation:
1. Combine avocados, cocoa powder, protein powder, honey, vanilla extract, and salt in a blender. Blend until smooth.
2. Transfer the mousse to serving dishes and refrigerate for at least 1 hour.
3. Before serving, garnish with chopped pistachios.

Storage Guidelines:

Refrigeration:
- Place the mousse in individual serving dishes, cover each tightly with plastic wrap, or transfer to an airtight container.
- The mousse can be stored in the refrigerator for up to 2-3 days. Ensure it's kept cold to maintain its texture and flavor.
- Garnish with pistachios just before serving to keep them crunchy.

Freezing is Not Recommended:
- While the mousse can technically be frozen, its texture may change upon thawing, potentially becoming less creamy and more icy.

Reheating:
- **No Reheating Required:** This dessert is meant to be served chilled. Remove it from the refrigerator a few minutes before serving to soften, enhancing its creamy texture slightly.
- If the mousse has been in the fridge for a couple of days, consider giving it a good stir or a quick re-blend to revive its creamy consistency if necessary.

Additional Tips:
- Consume the mousse within the recommended storage timeframe for optimal freshness and flavor.
- Since avocados oxidize and brown over time, adding honey or agave syrup not only sweetens the dish but also helps preserve the mousse's color. However, slight darkening over time is natural and doesn't indicate spoilage.
- Add the pistachio garnish before serving to maintain the nuts' crunchiness and flavor.

By adhering to these instructions, you can savor the delightful Chocolate Avocado Protein Mousse with Pistachios while ensuring it remains a tasty and nutritious treat!

A true confluence of taste and health, this Chocolate Avocado Protein Mousse is your guilt-free pass to indulge while sticking to your muscle-building regimen. Savor each spoon, knowing you're nourishing your body with every delightful bite!

50. Vanilla Protein Cheesecake with Berry Compote

Indulge in the delightful Vanilla Protein Cheesecake with Berry Compote, a delectable dessert where creamy cheesecake meets vibrant, tangy berries. This high-protein treat satisfies your sweet tooth while assisting in muscle building, making it a guilt-free indulgence.

Serving: 8
Prepping Time: 20 mins
Cook Time: 60 mins
Difficulty: Medium

Nutritional Facts (Per serving):
- Calories: 210
- Protein: 15g
- Fat: 10g
- Carbohydrates: 15g

Ingredients:
- 2 cups low-fat cream cheese
- 1 cup vanilla protein powder
- 1/2 cup granulated sweetener
- 2 large eggs
- 1 tsp vanilla extract
- 1/2 cup Greek yogurt
- 1 cup mixed berries (blueberries, raspberries)
- 1/4 cup berry compote
- Fresh mint leaves for garnish

Step-by-Step Preparation:
1. Preheat the oven and line the baking pan.
2. Blend cream cheese, protein powder, sweetener, eggs, and vanilla until smooth.
3. Pour into pan and bake.
4. Cool the cheesecake and refrigerate.
5. Top with mixed berries, compote, and mint before serving.

Storage Guidelines:

Refrigeration:

- Once the cheesecake has cooled completely, cover it tightly with plastic wrap or aluminum foil. You may also store individual slices in airtight containers.
- The cheesecake can be refrigerated for up to 5-7 days.
- Store the berry compote separately in a sealed container in the refrigerator.

Freezing:

- For more extended storage, you can freeze the cheesecake. Wrap it tightly to prevent freezer burn and store it in a freezer-safe container. It can be frozen for up to 2 months.
- Do not freeze the berry compote; prepare it fresh or use thawed berries when ready to serve.

Reheating:

- **Defrosting (if frozen):**
  - Place the frozen cheesecake in the refrigerator and allow it to thaw overnight.
  - Once thawed, it's ready to be served; no further reheating is needed.
- **Serving Tips:**
  - If you've stored the cheesecake in the refrigerator, you can serve it chilled directly.
  - Add the berry compote and fresh berries just before serving to maintain the freshness and flavor of the fruit.

Additional Tips:

- The cheesecake and compote should be stored separately to prevent the cake from becoming soggy.
- Consider consuming the cheesecake within the suggested storage periods for the best flavor and texture.
- When serving, consider adding a dollop of whipped cream or a sprinkle of powdered sugar for extra indulgence.

By following these storage and serving instructions, you can ensure that the Vanilla Protein Cheesecake with Berry Compote remains a delightful and appealing treat for you and your guests!

Savor the delightful balance of creamy cheesecake and tangy, fresh berries in this Vanilla Protein Cheesecake with Berry Compote. With every delicious bite, nourish your body and support your muscle-building goals without compromise.

51. Mocha Chocolate Coffee Protein Smoothie

Indulge in the rich and creamy Mocha Protein Smoothie, the perfect coffee, chocolate, and protein blend. This delightful beverage not only satiates your coffee and chocolate cravings but also fuels your muscles, making it a choice both delicious and nutritious.

Nutritional Facts (Per serving):
- Calories: 180
- Protein: 20g
- Fat: 2g
- Carbohydrates: 24g

Ingredients:

- 1 cup cold brewed coffee
- 1 scoop of chocolate protein powder
- 1 frozen banana
- 1/2 cup Greek yogurt
- 1 tbsp cocoa powder
- 1 tsp honey
- Ice cubes

Step-by-Step Preparation:

1. In a blender, combine all ingredients.
2. Blend until smooth and creamy.
3. Pour into glasses and serve immediately.

Storage Guidelines:

Refrigeration:
- If you have any leftover smoothie, pour it into an airtight container or bottle with a lid. Store in the refrigerator for up to 1 day. Over time, the smoothie may separate or lose its creamy consistency; a quick shake or stir should help recombine the ingredients.

Freezing:
- Pour the leftover smoothie into an ice cube tray and freeze it. Once frozen, transfer the smoothie cubes to a freezer bag. When ready for another smoothie, blend the cubes with liquid (like milk, coffee, or water) until it reaches the desired consistency.

Reheating/Serving:
- **Refrigerated Smoothie:**
  - Before serving a refrigerated smoothie, please give it a good shake or stir. If it has thickened too much in the fridge, consider blending it again with a bit of liquid to reach your preferred texture.
- **Frozen Smoothie Cubes:**
  - Blend the frozen smoothie cubes with additional liquid until you achieve a smooth, drinkable consistency. You may need to adjust the sweetness or flavor intensity with more honey, cocoa, or coffee, as freezing might dull the flavors slightly.

Additional Tips:
- This smoothie is best enjoyed immediately after blending to experience its full flavor and creamy texture.
- Adjust the thickness by adding more or fewer ice cubes or using more or less liquid. If desired, you may also adjust the sweetness with additional honey or a sugar substitute.

Following these instructions, you can enjoy the delightful Mocha Chocolate Coffee Protein Smoothie freshly blended or revive leftovers for a convenient, tasty, and nutritious treat!

Unwind with this velvety Mocha Protein Smoothie, a drink that doubles as both a muscle-building elixir and a chocolaty indulgence, striking a harmonious balance between health and pleasure.

52. Strawberry Protein Milkshake

Indulge guilt-free in a Strawberry Protein Milkshake, a delicious blend of strawberries and almonds. It provides delight to your tastebuds and protein for muscle-building, making it a perfect post-workout treat or a wholesome indulgence anytime.

Serving: 2
Prepping Time: 5 mins
Cook Time: 0 mins
Difficulty: Easy

Nutritional Facts (Per serving):
- Calories: 220
- Protein: 15g
- Fat: 6g
- Carbohydrates: 25g

Ingredients:
- 1 cup fresh strawberries
- 1 scoop vanilla protein powder
- 1 cup almond milk
- 1/2 cup vanilla Greek yogurt
- 1 tbsp honey
- Handful of ice cubes
- Sliced almonds for garnish

Step-by-Step Preparation:
1. Combine strawberries, protein powder, almond milk, Greek yogurt, honey, and ice in a blender.
2. Blend until smooth.
3. Pour into glasses and garnish with sliced almonds.

Storage Guidelines:

Refrigeration:
- If you have leftovers, pour the remaining milkshake into an airtight container and refrigerate for up to 1 day. The ingredients might settle and separate over time, so stir or shake the milkshake well before consumption.
- Ensure to cover the container tightly to prevent the milkshake from absorbing other odors from the fridge.

Freezing:
- Freezing is not recommended for this recipe, as it may alter the consistency and flavor of the milkshake upon thawing.

Serving:
- **From the Fridge:**
  - Remove the stored milkshake from the refrigerator.
  - Please give it a good stir or shake to mix any separated ingredients.
  - If it's too thick, try blending it again with more almond milk to reach the desired consistency.
  - Taste the milkshake and adjust the sweetness with more honey if necessary, as cold beverages often taste less sweet than those at room temperature.
  - Pour into a glass and garnish with fresh sliced almonds before serving.

Additional Tips:
- The Strawberry Protein Milkshake is best enjoyed immediately after blending to maintain the optimal flavor and consistency.
- If you plan on consuming the milkshake later, consider storing the components separately and mixing them just before serving to preserve the fresh taste and creamy texture.

By adhering to these storage and serving guidelines, you can savor the delightful and nutritious Strawberry Protein Milkshake while ensuring it retains its tasty and wholesome qualities!

Refresh and replenish with this sweet and satisfying Strawberry Protein Milkshake. With the richness of almonds and the sweetness of strawberries, it's a delightful dessert beverage that supports your muscle-building goals without compromise.

53. Chocolate Protein Brownies with Walnuts

Indulgence meets fitness with these Chocolate Protein Brownies infused with walnuts. These brownies are not just irresistibly chocolaty but are packed with protein, making them a perfect post-workout treat or a guilt-free indulgence for those muscle-building days.

Nutritional Facts (Per serving):

- Calories: 140
- Protein: 8g
- Fat: 7g
- Carbohydrates: 12g

Ingredients:

- 1 cup chocolate protein powder
- 1/2 cup unsweetened cocoa powder
- 1/4 cup coconut oil, melted
- 2 large eggs
- 1/2 cup almond milk
- 1/4 cup honey or maple syrup
- 1 tsp vanilla extract
- 1/2 cup chopped walnuts

Step-by-Step Preparation:

1. Preheat oven to 350°F (175°C) and grease an 8x8-inch baking pan.
2. In a bowl, mix protein powder and cocoa powder.
3. Add coconut oil, eggs, almond milk, honey, and vanilla. Mix until smooth.
4. Fold in the chopped walnuts.
5. Pour the batter into the prepared pan and spread evenly.
6. Bake for 20-25 minutes or until a toothpick comes out clean.
7. Let cool before slicing.

Storage Guidelines:

1. **Room Temperature:**
   - Store leftover brownies in an airtight container at room temperature for up to 3 days. Ensure the container is sealed tightly to prevent the brownies from drying out.
2. **Refrigeration:**
   - For longer shelf life, place the brownies in an airtight container and store them in the refrigerator for up to a week.
3. **Freezing:**
   - To freeze, individually wrap each brownie in plastic wrap and place them in a zip-top freezer bag. Label the bag with the date and type of brownies, which can be stored for up to 3 months.

Reheating:

- **From Room Temperature or Refrigerator:**
  - The brownies can be enjoyed at room temperature or slightly warmed. To warm them, place the brownies in a preheated oven at 350°F (175°C) for about 5 minutes or until they are warmed to your liking.
- **From Freezer:**
  - Thaw the frozen brownies at room temperature for several hours or overnight in the refrigerator. Once thawed, you can enjoy them as they are or warm them slightly in the oven, as mentioned above.

Additional Tips:

- Consider adding a moisture source, like a slice of bread or a piece of apple, to the airtight container if you store the brownies at room temperature, as this can help prevent them from drying out.
- When reheating multiple brownies, ensure they are spaced out evenly on the oven tray to allow for uniform heating.

Following these guidelines, you can enjoy the delightful and nutritious Chocolate Protein Brownies with Walnuts while preserving their moistness, flavor, and texture!

Sink your teeth into these delectably moist Chocolate Protein Brownies and enjoy the fusion of rich chocolate, crunchy walnuts, and muscle-boosting protein. An indulgent treat that supports your fitness journey!

54. Chocolate Peanut Butter Protein Cookies

Enjoy the divine chocolate and peanut butter combo in these delicious Protein Cookies! These treats are perfect for fitness enthusiasts who want to maintain taste while consuming healthy, muscle-building snacks.

- Serving: 12
- Prepping Time: 10 mins
- Cook Time: 12 mins
- Difficulty: Easy

Nutritional Facts (Per serving):

- Calories: 150
- Protein: 10g
- Fat: 8g
- Carbohydrates: 9g

Ingredients:

- 1 cup chocolate protein powder
- 1/2 cup natural peanut butter
- 1/4 cup honey
- 1 egg
- 1 tsp vanilla extract
- 1/2 tsp baking soda
- Chocolate chips (optional)

Step-by-Step Preparation:

1. Preheat oven to 350°F (180°C).
2. Mix protein powder, peanut butter, honey, egg, vanilla, and baking soda until smooth.
3. Form into balls and place on a baking sheet.
4. Flatten each ball and add chocolate chips if desired.
5. Bake for 10-12 minutes, let cool.

Storage Guidelines:

1. **Room Temperature:**
   - Once the cookies have cooled completely, store them in an airtight container. They can be kept at room temperature for up to one week. Ensure the container is in a cool, dry place to maintain the cookies' freshness and prevent them from becoming stale.
2. **Refrigeration:**
   - For extended freshness, consider refrigerating the cookies in an airtight container. They can be refrigerated for up to two weeks.
3. **Freezing:**
   - Place the cookies in a single layer inside a freezer-safe bag or container for more extended storage, separating layers with parchment paper to prevent sticking. Properly stored, they can last up to 3 months in the freezer.

Reheating:

- **From Room Temperature or Refrigerator:**
  - These cookies can be enjoyed at room temperature. If you prefer them slightly warm, you can heat them in a preheated oven at 350°F (180°C) for 3-5 minutes.
- **From Freezer:**
  - Allow the cookies to thaw at room temperature for about an hour. If you wish to warm them, use the oven method mentioned above after they have thawed.

Additional Tips:

- Ensure cookies are completely cool before storing to prevent condensation, which can lead to sogginess.
- Label the freezer bag or container with the date of storage to keep track of freshness.

Following these storage and reheating guidelines will help maintain the taste and texture of your Chocolate Peanut Butter Protein Cookies, allowing you to enjoy a nutritious and delightful snack whenever you crave it!

With these Chocolate Peanut Butter Protein Cookies, delight in a snack that's as nutritious as it is tasty! Perfect for an energy boost while you're on the move or post-workout refueling.

55. Almond Joy Protein Shake

Indulge guilt-free with the Almond Joy Protein Shake, combining the irresistible almonds, coconut, and chocolate flavors. This creamy delight is not just a treat to the palate but also a boost for muscle-building goals, making it a perfect indulgence.

Nutritional Facts (Per serving):
- Calories: 320
- Protein: 15g
- Fat: 18g
- Carbohydrates: 35g

Ingredients:

- 1/4 cup sliced almonds
- 2 scoops Primal Kitchen Chocolate Coconut Fuel
- 2 frozen bananas
- 1/4 cup unsweetened shredded coconut
- 1 tablespoon unsweetened cacao powder
- 1 tablespoon honey
- 2 cups almond milk
- 1 teaspoon almond extract

Step-by-Step Preparation:

1. In a blender, combine all ingredients.
2. Blend until the mixture is smooth and creamy.
3. Pour into glasses, garnish with extra almonds and coconut if desired, and serve immediately.

Storage Guidelines:

1. Refrigeration:

- If you have leftovers or need to store the shake for later consumption, pour it into an airtight container or a bottle with a tight-fitting lid and store it in the refrigerator. It should be consumed within 1-2 days for optimal freshness and taste.

2. Freezing:

- For more extended storage, you can freeze the shake. Pour it into an ice cube tray or a freezer-safe container, leaving some space at the top as the liquid will expand when it freezes. Frozen shake cubes can be stored for up to a month. When ready to consume, blend the frozen cubes until smooth.

Serving:

- **Refrigerated Shake:**
  - Before serving the refrigerated shake, please give it a good shake or stir, as separation is natural if the shake has thickened while in the refrigerator; you can adjust its consistency by blending it again with a bit more almond milk.

- **Frozen Shake:**
  - For frozen shakes, remove the amount you want to consume from the freezer and let it thaw slightly. Then, blend until it reaches a smooth consistency. Add a bit of almond milk to help it blend more efficiently and achieve your desired consistency.

Additional Tips:

- Always check the smell and consistency of the stored shake before consuming. If it smells off or shows signs of spoilage, it is safer to discard it.
- Consider garnishing with fresh almonds and coconut right before serving rather than before storage to maintain the texture and freshness of the garnish.

By following these storage and serving instructions, you can enjoy a delicious and nutritious Almond Joy Protein Shake at your convenience while maintaining its flavor and consistency!

End your workout with our Almond Joy Protein Shake, a delightful blend that supports your muscle building while satisfying your sweet tooth with wholesome ingredients.

56. Banana Nut Muffins

These Banana Nut Muffins are not only delightful but also filled with nourishing ingredients, offering a delightful way to indulge while still focusing on muscle-building. With a balanced blend of proteins and wholesome nutrients, each bite is a step towards a healthier indulgence.

Serving: 12
Prepping Time: 15 mins
Cook Time: 20 mins
Difficulty: Easy

Nutritional Facts (Per serving):
- Calories: 220
- Protein: 10g
- Fat: 15g
- Carbohydrates: 15g

Ingredients:

- 3 ripe bananas
- 1/4 cup melted butter
- 1/4 cup almond butter
- 1 teaspoon vanilla extract
- 1 cup almond flour
- 1/2 teaspoon baking soda
- 1/4 teaspoon salt
- 1/2 cup chopped walnuts or pecans
- 2 scoops of vanilla protein powder

Step-by-Step Preparation:

1. Preheat oven to 350°F (175°C).
2. In a bowl, mash bananas and mix in melted butter, almond butter, and vanilla extract.
3. Combine almond flour, baking soda, salt, and protein powder in another bowl.
4. Mix wet ingredients with dry ones, then fold in nuts.
5. Pour into muffin tins and bake for 20 minutes or until a toothpick comes out clean.

Storage Guidelines:

1. **Room Temperature:**
   - Store the muffins in an airtight container at room temperature. They should stay fresh for up to 2 days. Ensure the container is sealed tightly to prevent the muffins from drying out.
2. **Refrigeration:**
   - Store the muffins in the refrigerator in an airtight container for a longer shelf life. They will stay fresh for up to a week. To prevent them from drying out, you should place a piece of paper towel at the bottom of the container to absorb excess moisture.
3. **Freezing:**
   - If you wish to store them for an extended period, wrap each muffin individually in plastic wrap and then place them in a zip-top freezer bag. Label the bag with the date, and the muffins can be frozen for up to 3 months.

Reheating:

- **From Room Temperature:**
  - Muffins stored at room temperature or in the refrigerator do not necessarily need to be reheated. However, if you prefer them warm, you can heat them in the microwave for 10-15 seconds.
- **From Freezer:**
  - Thaw the frozen muffins at room temperature or in the refrigerator overnight. Once thawed, if you wish to serve them warm, heat them in the microwave for 15-20 seconds or until they reach your desired temperature.

Serving Tip:

- Consider warming the muffins slightly before serving, as it can help to enhance their flavor and make them taste more like they've just been baked.

Note:
- Always check the muffins for signs of spoilage before consuming, like an off-smell, mold, or any other unusual appearance. If in doubt, it's safer to discard them.

Following these guidelines, you can enjoy your Banana Nut Muffins while maintaining their freshness and delicious taste!

Indulge smartly with these Banana Nut Muffins, a sweet treat designed to align with your muscle-building goals while satisfying your dessert cravings with a delightful taste and texture.

57. Matcha Green Tea Smoothie With Berries Topping

Delight in the refreshing Matcha Green Tea Smoothie crowned with vibrant berries! This concoction is a perfect blend of antioxidants and proteins, offering a nutrient-rich indulgence that supports muscle gains while satisfying your sweet tooth with its delectable flavors.

Serving: 2
Prepping Time: 10 mins
Cook Time: 0 mins
Difficulty: Easy

Nutritional Facts (Per serving):
- Calories: 180
- Protein: 15g
- Fat: 3g
- Carbohydrates: 26g

Ingredients:
- 1 teaspoon matcha green tea powder
- 1 scoop vanilla protein powder
- 1 cup unsweetened almond milk
- 1 frozen banana
- 1/2 cup mixed berries for topping
- 1 tablespoon honey (optional)
- Ice cubes

Step-by-Step Preparation:
1. Combine matcha, protein powder, almond milk, banana, and ice until smooth in a blender.
2. Pour the smoothie into glasses.
3. Top with mixed berries and drizzle with honey if desired.

Storage Guidelines:

1. Short-term:
- If you can't consume the smoothie immediately, storing it in the refrigerator for up to 24 hours is recommended. Use a glass with a tight-fitting lid or cover it with plastic wrap to maintain freshness.

2. Not Suitable for Long-Term Storage:
- Due to the nature of the ingredients, this smoothie is best enjoyed fresh and unsuitable for long-term storage. Extended storage might lead to separating ingredients and degradation of flavor and nutrients.

Serving:

- **Re-stir or Blend:**
  - If the smoothie has been stored and the ingredients have separated, give it a good stir or a quick blend before serving to restore its creamy consistency.
- **Temperature:**
  - This smoothie is best served cold. If it has warmed up during storage, try to chill it again before serving, or add a few ice cubes for an extra refreshing touch.
- **Adding the Topping:**
  - If you've stored the smoothie without the berry topping, add the mixed berries and optional honey drizzle right before serving to maintain the freshness and texture of the berries.

Additional Tips:

- **Adjust Sweetness:**
  - The sweetness of the smoothie may change slightly after storage. Taste it before serving, and if necessary, adjust the sweetness by adding a little more honey or your preferred sweetener.
- **Serve Immediately After Preparation:**
  - For the best taste and nutritional value, consuming the smoothie as soon as possible after preparation is advised.

Following these guidelines, you can enjoy your Matcha Green Tea Smoothie with Berries Topping while ensuring it remains a delightful, refreshing, and nutritious treat!

Sip your way to muscle gain with this delightful Matcha Green Tea Smoothie! Its tantalizing taste and nutrient profile make it a fantastic choice for those looking to enjoy a guilt-free, muscle-supporting indulgence.

58. Banana Peanut Butter Protein Shake

Unveil the ultimate muscle-building indulgence with the Banana Peanut Butter Protein Shake! This thick, satisfying drink is a powerhouse of energy, combining the goodness of bananas and peanut butter with the robustness of oats and the sweetness of agave, all while supporting your muscle gains seamlessly.

Nutritional Facts (Per serving):
- Calories: 320
- Protein: 18g
- Fat: 10g
- Carbohydrates: 45g

Ingredients:

- 2 ripe bananas
- 2 tablespoons peanut butter
- 1/2 cup rolled oats
- 1 tablespoon agave syrup
- 1 scoop of chocolate protein powder
- 1 cup almond milk
- Ice cubes
- Mint leaves for garnish

Step-by-Step Preparation:

1. Blend bananas, peanut butter, oats, agave syrup, protein powder, and almond milk until smooth.
2. Add ice cubes and blend again until frosty.
3. Pour into glasses and garnish with mint.

Storage Guidelines:

1. **Short-term:**
   - If you aren't consuming the shake immediately, it's best to refrigerate and finish it within 24 hours. Use a container with a tight-sealing lid or cover the glass with plastic wrap to keep the shake fresh.
2. **Not Suitable for Long-Term Storage:**
   - This shake is formulated for immediate or short-term consumption. It's recommended to store for only a short time, as the ingredients can separate, and the shake may lose its freshness and texture.

Serving:

- **Shake Well Before Consuming:**
  - If the shake has been refrigerated, the ingredients might settle or separate. Before consuming, please give it a thorough shake or a quick re-blend to restore its creamy consistency.
- **Temperature:**
  - This shake is best served chilled. If it has warmed up while stored, consider adding a few ice cubes or briefly refrigerating to achieve a cold, refreshing temperature.
- **Garnish:**
  - Add the fresh mint leaves garnish right before you serve the shake to maintain the mint's vibrant color and aroma.

Additional Tips:

- **Adjust Sweetness:**
  - The sweetness of the shake can vary based on the ripeness of bananas or if it's been stored. Taste and adjust sweetness by adding more agave syrup if desired before serving.
- **Freshness is Key:**
  - Like most protein shakes, this shake is best when consumed fresh after blending to retain its texture, flavor, and nutrient content.

Following these storage and serving recommendations, your Banana Peanut Butter Protein Shake will remain a delightful and nutritious treat, ready to support your muscle-building efforts whenever desired.

Indulge guilt-free with the Banana Peanut Butter Protein Shake, a delightful concoction designed for muscle-building support and sublime flavor, making it an indispensable addition to your high-protein dessert and beverage collection.

59. Coconut White Chocolate Protein Truffles

Savor the delightful coconut and white chocolate combination with these irresistible Protein Truffles! Perfectly crafted to satisfy your sweet tooth while providing a protein boost, these truffles are a lovely treat that supports your muscle-building goals without compromising on taste.

Serving: 15
Prepping Time: 20 mins
Cook Time: 0 mins
Difficulty: Medium

Nutritional Facts (Per serving):
- Calories: 130
- Protein: 5g
- Fat: 9g
- Carbohydrates: 8g

Ingredients:
- 1 cup unsweetened shredded coconut
- 1/2 cup vanilla protein powder
- 1/4 cup almond flour
- 1/4 cup melted coconut oil
- 1/4 cup honey
- 1/2 teaspoon vanilla extract
- 1/4 teaspoon salt
- 1/2 cup white chocolate chips

Step-by-Step Preparation:
1. Mix coconut, protein powder, almond flour, coconut oil, honey, vanilla extract, and salt until well combined.
2. Form the mixture into small balls and place them on a lined tray.
3. Melt white chocolate and dip each truffle into it, then put it back on the tray.
4. Refrigerate until set.

Storage Guidelines:

1. **Refrigeration:**
   - Store the truffles in the refrigerator in an airtight container, separating layers with parchment paper to prevent sticking. They should be consumed within 7 to 10 days for optimal freshness and taste.
2. **Freezing for Longer Shelf Life:**
   - Place the truffles in a freezer-safe, airtight container with parchment paper between layers for extended storage. They can be frozen for up to 2 months. Ensure they are correctly sealed to prevent freezer burn.

Serving:

- **Thawing (if frozen):**
  - Remove the desired number of truffles from the freezer and let them thaw in the refrigerator for a few hours before serving. Avoid thawing at room temperature to prevent melting and loss of shape.
- **Serving Temperature:**
  - These truffles are best enjoyed chilled. Serving them straight from the refrigerator or shortly after thawing maximizes their flavor and texture.

Additional Tips:

- **Handling:**
  - Handle the truffles carefully, as they might be delicate and can lose shape if pressed or squeezed too hard.
- **Variation:**
  - For a different flavor profile, you may experiment with adding a bit of citrus zest or changing the type of protein powder. However, altering ingredients may affect the storage life and texture of the truffles.

Following these storage and serving recommendations ensures that your Coconut White Chocolate Protein Truffles remain a delightful, indulgent treat that aligns with your muscle-building dietary goals.

Dive into the world of indulgent treats with the Coconut White Chocolate Protein Truffles. A dessert that's not only delightful but also packed with protein, perfect for anyone looking to build muscle while enjoying delicious treats!

60. Vanilla Protein Donuts with Chocolate Glaze

Indulge in Vanilla Protein Donuts with Chocolate Glaze, the perfect blend of delectable sweetness and essential protein. This delightful treat is ideal for satisfying your sweet cravings while adhering to your muscle-building dietary goals.

Serving 12
Prepping Time 15 mins
Cook Time 12 mins
Difficulty Easy

Nutritional Facts (Per serving):
- Calories: 210
- Protein: 10g
- Fat: 12g
- Carbohydrates: 15g

Ingredients:
- 1 cup vanilla protein powder
- 1 cup almond flour
- 1 tsp baking powder
- 1/4 cup Greek yogurt
- 2 large eggs
- 1/4 cup almond milk
- 2 tbsp coconut oil, melted
- For glaze: 1/2 cup dark chocolate, melted

Step-by-Step Preparation:
1. Mix dry ingredients; then add yogurt, eggs, milk, and oil.
2. Pour batter into donut molds and bake at 350°F for 12 minutes.
3. Once cooled, dip each donut into melted chocolate.

Storage Guidelines:

1. **Refrigeration:**
   - Place the donuts in an airtight container, separated by parchment paper to prevent them from sticking together, and refrigerate. Consume within 3-5 days for the best freshness and taste.
2. **Freezing for Longer Shelf Life:**
   - The donuts can be frozen if you want to store them for an extended period. Please place them in a freezer-safe, airtight container with parchment paper between layers. They can be frozen for up to 1 month. Ensure they're sealed well to avoid freezer burn.

Reheating:

- **From the Refrigerator:**
  - For a slightly warm donut, you can microwave each on a microwave-safe plate for 10-15 seconds. However, avoid overheating, as the chocolate glaze might melt too much.
- **From the Freezer:**
  - Thaw the donuts in the refrigerator overnight. Once thawed, if you desire a slightly warm donut, microwave as directed above.

Serving Tips:

- For added flair, consider sprinkling some powdered sugar or chopped nuts over the chocolate glaze before serving.
- Serve the donuts with a cold glass of almond milk or your preferred beverage for satisfying treat.

Additional Tips:

- **Storing Extras:**
  - If you have extra chocolate glaze left, you can store it in the refrigerator in an airtight container for up to a week. Reheat gently in the microwave (in short bursts) or over a double boiler when needed.

By following these storage, reheating, and serving recommendations, you can ensure your Vanilla Protein Donuts with Chocolate Glaze remain a mouth-watering treat that's ready to enjoy whenever the craving strikes!

These Vanilla Protein Donuts with Chocolate Glaze offer a sublime experience for your taste buds, combining the classic flavors of vanilla and chocolate with the added benefit of protein, making them a delightful and guilt-free indulgence.

Note:

⭐⭐⭐⭐⭐ **Leave a Review** ⭐⭐⭐⭐⭐
As an independent author with a small marketing budget, reviews are my livelihood on this platform. If you enjoyed this book, I'd appreciate it if you could leave your honest feedback. I read EVERY single review because I love the feedback from MY readers!
If you do not know what to write, you can simply choose a star rating (one to five stars), which only takes a moment.

Thank you in advance for leaving a rating or review. We appreciate you!

1. **FIND** this book on Amazon
2. **SCROLL** down to the reviews
3. **SELECT**

Write a customer review

Chapter 8: Meal Plans and Fitness Tips

Embarking on a high-protein journey isn't just about the food you consume. It's a holistic approach that includes structuring your meals, incorporating exercise, and tracking your progress. This chapter will provide a foundation for crafting a balanced meal plan, combining it efficiently with workouts, and monitoring your journey to ensure you're moving toward your goals. By the end of this chapter, you'll not only have weekly meal plans at your disposal but also be equipped with knowledge on how to marry these meals with an effective workout routine. Let's get started!

Weekly Meal Plans:

It's essential to plan to ensure a balanced intake of protein, carbs, and fats. Crafting a balanced meal plan is paramount. We've chosen meals from the preceding chapters to create a balanced weekly plan. Remember, consistency is key. Here's a sample:

Week .... Month ....

Day	Breakfast	Lunch	Dinner	Snack	Dessert	Note
Mon	Muscle Morning Protein Smoothie (Recipe 01)	Grilled Chicken Caesar Salad Protein Bowl (Recipe 14)	Beef Steak with Chimichurri Sauce (Recipe 25)	Spicy Tuna Stuffed Avocado Halves (Recipe 37)	Chocolate Avocado Protein Mousse with Pistachios (Recipe 49)	WATER INTAKE ○○○○○○
Tue	Chia Seed Protein Pudding with Fresh Berries (Recipe 07)	Bulking Up Chickpea & Spinach Curry (Recipe 17)	Lamb Chops with Rosemary and Garlic (Recipe 28)	Baked Kale Chips With Parmesan (Recipe 39)	Vanilla Protein Cheesecake with Berry Compote (Recipe 50)	WATER INTAKE ○○○○○○
Wed	Morning Glory Protein Pancakes (Recipe 03)	Protein-Packed Grilled Salmon Salad (Recipe 18)	Traditional Spanish paella with seafood and chicken (Recipe 26)	Greek Yogurt and Dill Dip (Recipe 41)	Mocha Chocolate Coffee Protein Smoothie (Recipe 51)	WATER INTAKE ○○○○○○
Thu	Chia Protein Overnight Oats (Recipe 04)	Muscle Building Beef and Broccoli Stir Fry (Recipe 16)	Garlic Butter Shrimp Pasta (Recipe 27)	Protein-Packed Guacamole With Hemp Seeds (Recipe 44)	Strawberry Protein Milkshake (Recipe 52)	WATER INTAKE ○○○○○○
Fri	High-Protein Blueberry Quinoa Muffins (Recipe 05)	Lean Muscle Building Shrimp & Quinoa Bowl (Recipe 19)	Miso Glazed Salmon with Bok Choy (Recipe 29)	Roasted Red Pepper Hummus (Recipe 38)	Chocolate Protein Brownies with Walnuts (Recipe 53)	WATER INTAKE ○○○○○○
Sat	Vanilla Whey Protein Waffles (Recipe 10)	Chargrilled Chicken & Vegetable Skewers (Recipe 20)	Lentil and Sausage Stew (Recipe 30)	Cottage Cheese and Pineapple Bowl (Recipe 42)	Banana Peanut Butter Protein Shake (Recipe 58)	WATER INTAKE ○○○○○○
Sun	Lean Muscle Avocado Toast with Turkey Bacon (Recipe 11)	High-Protein Vegan Buddha Bowl (Recipe 21)	Thai Green Curry with Chicken (Recipe 36)	Quinoa Tabbouleh Salad (Recipe 45)	Vanilla Protein Donuts with Chocolate Glaze (Recipe 60)	WATER INTAKE ○○○○○○

[...Continue for other days...]

This table provides a balanced spread of the recipes from the chapters, ensuring variety throughout the week. Adjustments can be made based on personal preferences or nutritional needs.

Remember, variety is the key. Switch up the protein sources and accompanying sides to ensure a diverse range of nutrients and avoid monotony. You can mix and match recipes from earlier chapters, ensuring each day is as nutritious as it is delicious.

Tips for Combining Exercise with a High-Protein Diet:

1. Timing is Essential:

- **Pre-Workout:** Consume a balanced meal 1-3 hours before your workout, ensuring it contains a moderate amount of protein, healthy fats, and carbs. This tips provides sustained energy during your exercise.
- **Post-Workout:** After exercising, consume a protein-rich meal or shake within 30 minutes to an hour. This period is known as the "anabolic window," where muscle protein synthesis is elevated.

2. Distribute Protein Intake:

- Aim to spread your protein intake evenly throughout the day. Consuming protein in each meal ensures a constant supply of amino acids, which is crucial for muscle repair and growth.

3. Opt for High-Quality Protein Sources:

- Not all protein sources are equal. Focus on consuming complete protein sources containing all nine essential amino acids. Examples include lean meats, dairy, eggs, and specific plant-based options like quinoa and tofu.

4. Stay Hydrated:

- A high-protein diet can put more strain on your kidneys. Combine this with sweating from exercise, and the need for hydration increases. Ensure you're drinking enough water throughout the day.

5. Monitor Your Energy Levels:

- While protein is vital, don't neglect carbohydrates, especially if you're engaging in high-intensity or endurance exercises. Carbs are the body's primary energy source during these activities.

6. Listen to Your Body:

- If you feel more fatigued than usual or struggle to recover after workouts, you may need to adjust your protein intake or overall caloric consumption.

7. Strength Training is Key:

- A high-protein diet shines best when combined with resistance training. Lifting weights breaks down muscle fibers, and protein aids in repairing and growing them back stronger.

8. Incorporate Rest Days:

- Remember that recovery is when the actual muscle-building occurs. Ensure you have adequate rest days in your routine to allow muscles to repair fully.

9. Consider Supplements:

- If you're struggling to get enough protein from whole foods, consider adding a high-quality protein powder or BCAA (Branched-Chain Amino Acids) supplement. These can support muscle growth and recovery.

10. Limit Processed Foods:

- While reaching for processed high-protein bars or shakes is tempting, focus on getting most of your protein from whole food sources. They provide additional essential nutrients and are generally healthier.

11. Adjust as Needed:

- As you progress in your fitness journey, your protein needs might change. Regularly assess your goals and adjust your diet and exercise routine accordingly.

12. Consult a Professional:

- If you're unsure about the specifics of your diet or exercise regimen, consider consulting a registered dietitian or a personal trainer. They can provide personalized advice tailored to your needs.

Combining exercise with a high-protein diet effectively requires a balance of proper timing, quality nutrients, and adequate training. By following these tips, you can ensure you're maximizing the benefits of both for optimal health and muscle gain.

Tracking Your Progress:

Consistent tracking of your progress is not only motivating but also provides valuable data to refine your approach. Here are detailed methods and insights on how to effectively track your progress:

1. Before and After Photos:

- **Purpose:** Visual evidence of your transformation over time.
- **How-To:** Wear similar clothing and stand in the exact location with consistent lighting. Take photos from the front, side, and back views.
- **Frequency:** Take photos every 2-4 weeks to monitor changes.

2. Body Measurements:

- **Purpose:** Quantify changes in size and shape of different body parts.
- **How-To:** Use a flexible measuring tape.
  - **Waist:** Measure around the narrowest part, usually just above the belly button.
  - **Hips:** Measure around the widest part of your buttocks.
  - **Chest:** Measure around the fullest part, under the armpits.
  - **Biceps:** Measure around the thickest part of the upper arm.
  - **Thighs:** Measure around the thickest part of the upper thigh.
- **Frequency:** Every 4 weeks.

3. Strength Progress:

- **Purpose:** Track how your strength is increasing over time.
- **How-To:** Keep a workout log, noting down exercises, weights used, sets, and reps.
- **Frequency:** After every workout.

4. Set Clear Goals:

- Whether it's gaining a certain amount of muscle mass, lifting a specific weight, or achieving a particular body fat percentage, clear goals will guide your journey and provide motivation.

5. Dietary Log:

- **Purpose:** Ensure consistent dietary habits aligned with your goals.
- **How-To:** Use apps or a simple journal. Record everything you eat and drink, including portion sizes.
- **Note:** Be honest. Even if you have a cheat day, jot it down. This step can provide insights into patterns or triggers for unhealthy eating.
- **Frequency:** Daily.

6. Weight Tracking:
- **Purpose:** Monitor overall weight changes.
- **How-To:** Use a digital scale. Weigh yourself at the same time of day, ideally in the morning after using the bathroom and before eating.
- **Frequency:** Weekly. Daily weighing can be influenced by water retention, food intake, and other factors, which can be misleading.

7. Performance Metrics:
- **Purpose:** Track endurance, speed, or other performance-related metrics.
- **How-To:** Depending on your goals, you might track running times over a certain distance, the number of push-ups or pull-ups you can do in one go, or how long you can hold a plank.
- **Frequency:** Every 2-4 weeks, depending on the metric.

8. Feedback from Peers:
- **Purpose:** Sometimes, others notice changes before you do.
- **How-To:** Periodically ask friends or gym buddies if they notice any changes in your physique or performance. Their feedback can be encouraging and provide a different perspective.

9. Journaling:
- **Purpose:** Monitor feelings, energy levels, and overall well-being.
- **How-To:** Keep a daily diary, noting down how you feel, energy levels, sleep quality, and any other relevant factors. Over time, patterns linking diet or exercise changes with how you think may emerge.
- **Frequency:** Daily or as often as needed.

Remember, while all these tracking methods provide valuable insights, avoiding becoming overly obsessed with numbers is essential. They are tools to help you on your journey, but your well-being, how you feel, and enjoying the process are just as important. Combining a high-protein diet with the proper exercise regimen and tracking mechanisms can be a potent formula for achieving muscle gain and improved body composition. Stay committed, be patient, and the results will follow.

Things to focus on for progress tracking:

1. Document Your Workouts: For your exercise routine, keep track of the type of exercises, sets, reps, and weights lifted. This not only helps you see your progression but also ensures you're challenging yourself appropriately.

2. Strength and Performance: Keep a record of your strength gains and performance improvements. Are you lifting heavier weights, completing more reps, or running faster? These indicators show that your body is adapting positively.

3. Nutrition Logs: Record what you eat, including portion sizes and macronutrient breakdown. This step helps ensure you're meeting your nutritional goals and can identify areas for improvement.

4. Energy Levels and Mood: Pay attention to how you feel throughout the day. Increased energy levels and improved mood can be positive indicators that your diet and exercise regimen are working for you.

5. Sleep Quality: Adequate rest is crucial for recovery and muscle growth. Track your sleep patterns to ensure you're getting the recommended 7-9 hours of quality sleep per night.

6. Consistency Check: Assess how consistently you're sticking to your meal and workout plans. Consistency is often the key to long-term success.

7. Set SMART Goals: Create Specific, Measurable, Achievable, Relevant, and Time-bound (SMART) goals. Having clear objectives can help you stay focused and motivated.

8. Celebrate Milestones: Acknowledge and celebrate your achievements, no matter how small. Reward yourself for reaching milestones to maintain motivation.

9. Regular Assessments: Plan regular assessments, such as every 4-6 weeks, to review your progress and make necessary adjustments to your diet and exercise routine.

10. Seek Feedback: Don't hesitate to seek feedback from fitness professionals, trainers, or experienced individuals. They can provide valuable insights and suggestions.

11. Stay Patient: Progress may not always be linear. There may be plateaus or setbacks, but patience and consistency are crucial for long-term success.

12. Reevaluate Your Goals: Periodically reassess your fitness goals to ensure they align with your current aspirations and lifestyle.

By consistently tracking your progress using these methods, you'll gain valuable insights into your fitness journey, enabling you to make informed decisions, stay motivated, and ultimately achieve your desired results. Remember that everyone's progress is unique, so be patient and stay committed to your goals.

Conclusion:

As you turn this final page, it's essential to remember that your dedication to a healthier and stronger body brought you here. The journey through this "High Protein Cookbook for Muscle Gain" has equipped you with powerful knowledge, tools, and delicious recipes.

This isn't just another cookbook—it's a comprehensive guide, bridging the gap between fitness and nutrition. We began by demystifying the role of protein, underscoring its critical importance for muscle growth, recovery, and overall health. Each chapter thereafter unfurled an array of recipes—from hearty breakfasts to savory dinners and even indulgent yet protein-packed desserts—all designed with one goal: to help you reach your peak physical potential.

Imagine a lifestyle where every meal fuels your ambitions, where each bite brings you one step closer to your fitness goals. Visualize the muscles you've worked so hard for, being nourished and growing with the aid of each dish you've learned to prepare from this very cookbook. Feel the energy, strength, and vitality that comes from feeding your body the very best.

But the journey doesn't end here. The true adventure lies in applying what you've learned. Start today—prepare a recipe from this book and pair it with your workout. Document your journey, whether it's through photos, a diary, or sharing with friends and the broader community. Engage with others on platforms like Instagram or Twitter using #HighProteinMuscleJourney, creating a ripple of inspiration. Continue to educate yourself, innovate with these recipes, and remain steadfast on your path to greatness.

Printed in Great Britain
by Amazon